THE STUDY OF
TOTALITARIANISM
AN INDUCTIVE APPROACH

A Guide for Teachers

Bulletin Number 37

THE
STUDY OF
TOTALITARIANISM
AN INDUCTIVE APPROACH
A GUIDE FOR
TEACHERS

HOWARD D. MEHLINGER

Indiana University

NATIONAL COUNCIL FOR THE SOCIAL STUDIES

A DEPARTMENT OF THE NATIONAL EDUCATION ASSOCIATION

1201 Sixteenth Street Northwest, Washington D. C. 20036

Price $2.00

The National Council for the Social Studies is the Department of Social Studies of the National Education Association of the United States. It is the professional organization of teachers of social studies. It holds a series of meetings each year and publishes materials of significance to those interested in instruction in this field. Membership in the National Council carries with it a subscription to the Council's official journal, *Social Education*, the monthly magazine for social studies teachers, and the yearbook. In addition, the Council publishes bulletins, pamphlets, and other materials of practical use for teachers of the social studies. Membership dues are $9.00 a year. Applications for membership and orders for the purchase of publications should be made to the Executive Secretary, 1201 Sixteenth Street, N.W., Washington, D.C. 20036.

Foreword

What is totalitarianism? The answer to this question is thoroughly treated in a stimulating and highly informative publication by William Ebenstein entitled *Totalitarianism: New Perspectives.* Co-sponsored by the National Council for the Social Studies and the American Jewish Committee, *Totalitarianism: New Perspectives* was published in 1962 by Holt, Rinehart, and Winston. It is still the definitive volume on this subject for social studies teachers.

How should one approach the teaching of totalitarianism in the classroom? The answer to this question is found in the excellent guide you now have in your hands. Here Howard D. Mehlinger not only deals with methods but he provides the teacher with source materials, lesson plans, reading lists and other valuable materials. It is a practical volume which should prove as useful in the field of techniques as Ebenstein's has in the field of theory and background.

With this publication, as with the earlier one, the National Council for the Social Studies acknowledges the assistance of Dr. John Slawson and Max Birnbaum of the American Jewish Committee. It was through their efforts that some of the financial aid for this project was obtained from the Joseph Fels Foundation.

We also extend our thanks to the Foreign Relations Project of the North Central Association for making it possible for Howard D. Mehlinger, a member of their staff at the time manuscript was prepared, to devote the necessary time to prepare the manuscript.

To Dr. Mehlinger go the thanks and congratulations of the Council for a job which goes far "beyond the call of duty." Teachers who use this guide, we sincerely believe, will join with us in our thanks and their students will benefit by being better equipped to live in a fast-changing world that contains ideologies which often conflict with those of our own country.

William H. Hartley, *President*
National Council for the Social Studies

Acknowledgments

I wish to express my appreciation to a number of individuals who have brought this guide to completion. Mr. Merrill F. Hartshorn of the National Council for the Social Studies and Mr. Max Birnbaum of the American Jewish Committee suggested the guide and provided for its publication. Mr. James M. Becker, Director of the NCA Foreign Relations Project, and others on the Project staff offered continuous support. The guide profited from the critical review of Professor John Thompson, Indiana University.

A special debt of gratitude is due Miss Martha J. Porter, a Foreign Relations Project staff member. Miss Porter not only edited the entire manuscript but also suggested a number of ideas which were included in portions of the unit. What strengths the book may have are due primarily to her gentle but critical touch.

Finally, I wish to mention my wife Carolee, who typed the manuscript and tolerated my preoccupation during its preparation.

Howard D. Mehlinger

Table of Contents

FOREWORD .... WILLIAM H. HARTLEY   vii

ACKNOWLEDGMENTS .... HOWARD D. MEHLINGER   ix

I. INTRODUCTION   1

II. FACETS OF TOTALITARIANISM: NINE GENERALIZATIONS

Generalization No. 1: *The nature of the political system which will evolve in any nation depends in part upon the values held by its citizens.*   8

Generalization No. 2: *All societies cope with the problem of individual freedom versus public control. No contemporary society can be judged to be either completely free or completely totalitarian. Nevertheless, nations differ markedly and significantly in their attitudes toward and treatment of the relationship between freedom and control; these differences form identifiable but rather loosely defined and fluctuating patterns.*   17

Generalization No. 3: *Totalitarian regimes depend upon a command mechanism to run their economic systems*   23

Generalization No. 4: *Totalitarian states are characterized by single party political systems. Party membership is limited to those who are willing to be unquestionably loyal to the party leaders. Party interest and control encompasses all aspects of the society.*   37

Generalization No. 5: *Totalitarian systems tend to fall to the control of single leaders. These leaders are then made out to be almost superhuman.*   49

Generalization No. 6: *Totalitarian regimes are characterized by a commitment to a specific ideology. The ideology serves the state by defining the past, explaining the present, and predicting the future. It establishes guidelines for remolding society in the image held by the rulers. To the degree that the ideology is accepted by the mass of population, it can inspire dedication and loyalty to the regime.*   54

Generalization No. 7: *A totalitarian state seeks to subordinate all social institutions to the control of the state and thereby removes all possible challengers to its control. No human activity is without interest to totalitarian rulers. To control the behavior of its citizens, totalitarian regimes recognize no limits to the means which may be employed to achieve their ends.* 60

Generalization No. 8: *The type of totalitarianism which develops in a country is conditioned primarily by that nation's unique historical experience. The nature of the ideology, the level of economic development, and the degree of democratic experience are significant factors in explaining the origins and development of any totalitarian state* 93

Generalization No. 9: *Totalitarianism is a political, social and economic system which uses any means available to subject the individual to the goals and leadership of the state.* 100

III. SUGGESTIONS FOR FURTHER READING 103

THE STUDY OF
TOTALITARIANISM
AN INDUCTIVE APPROACH

A Guide for Teachers

CHAPTER I

Introduction

The American Declaration of Independence was, to the Western world of the eighteenth century, a most subversive document. It dared to proclaim what until then had been only the ideas of a few philosophers, namely that "all men are created equal," that men are born with "certain inalienable rights," that governments are formed for the purpose of securing these rights, and that whenever a government acts in violation of these rights "it is the right of the people to alter or abolish it." It is little wonder that European monarchs viewed these ideas with suspicion and hostility. They had neither gained office nor maintained it by popular support. Subsequent events showed that their fears were justified: in 1789, the quest for liberty, equality, and fraternity was proclaimed by the French Revolution, toppled the monarchy, established a republic, and foreshadowed all the social upheavals of the nineteenth century.

Throughout the nineteenth century, liberalism, democracy, and republicanism gained popular favor. Those monarchs who were able to preserve their thrones found it necessary to tailor their systems to accommodate democratic ideas. Although Europe as well as the rest of the world was dominated by authoritarian government, it appeared that time was on the side of the democracies and that democracy was the "wave of the future."

The experiences of the twentieth century, however, are not reassuring to the advocates of democracy. Successful democratic systems are still rare. Furthermore, what seemed to be a favorable democratic current has been obstructed by a new political form—totalitarianism. What makes totalitarianism so effective is its ability to capitalize on democratic slogans to achieve its ends while it drains them of their meaning. Whereas nineteenth-cen-

1

tury liberalism stressed individual freedom as a bundle of privileges to be guarded against the encroachment of the state, Mussolini argued that individuals acquire real meaning only when they become committed to furthering the goals of the state. Whereas Thomas Jefferson believed that the state exists merely to prevent individuals from doing harm to each other, otherwise leaving them free to regulate their own lives, the modern totalitarian believes that all activities of citizens are the proper concern of the state.

Since the rise of totalitarian states constitutes the most important political phenomenon of the twentieth century, it deserves attention in the social studies curriculum. Although totalitarianism is often treated implicitly through a study of its various manifestations, there has been little effort to provide meaning to the concept itself. The reasons for this neglect may lie in the comparatively recent origin of the term, or in the fact that it is used more by professional political scientists than by the lay public, and has not yet penetrated the textbooks.

As a concept, totalitarianism may be treated in the same manner as such concepts as imperialism, socialism, or nationalism. Since these terms are better known and understood by secondary school teachers, they lend themselves to special treatment. World history teachers, for example, are more likely to present imperialism as a phenomenon of the late nineteenth and early twentieth centuries than they are to consider in detail every type of imperialism which existed. While acknowledging that British imperialism differed from French, Russian, Belgian, German, or American imperialism, the teacher usually tends to concentrate on those factors which were similar and which give meaning to the concept, rather than studying each example in detail. An understanding of the concept enables a student to organize and make sense of the material he encounters from different examples. On the other hand, successive treatments of isolated experiences remain just that for most students.

Unlike imperialism, however, totalitarianism is seldom treated conceptually by social studies teachers. Instead, teachers usually provide detailed treatment of one or more states that exhibit totalitarian characteristics without actually examining those characteristics which differentiate totalitarian, authoritarian and democratic states. Those nations chosen for special study are invariably those that pose the greatest danger to American interests at a given point in time. Thus, in the early 1940's, German, Italian, and Japanese totalitarian systems were studied because these nations were our enemies in World War II. What similarities were stressed among the three derived largely from the fact that they were our enemies—and, it followed, that the rulers were cruel and the people not to be trusted. At the same time, totalitarian states allied with the United States—notably the USSR— appeared in an altogether different light, even though they shared many of the same characteristics. Thus, Russians were courageous, hard-working, and although not democratic certainly moving in that direction.

Now, of course, the world situation has changed; and it is the USSR which poses the gravest military threat to the United States. Consequently, in the 1950's and 60's, public support has arisen for offering courses or units on communism in order to inform American students about this danger. In some cases units on communism and the USSR are taught as fairly as is possible, given the problems of objectivity in dealing with controversial issues; in far too many cases, however, such units are little more than "know your enemy" exercises in political indoctrination scarcely flattering to American education.

When a topic is selected because it relates to a real or imagined threat, one can hardly expect the subject to receive fair treatment. If, on the other hand, the same topic is selected because of its crucial importance to an undersanding of a period in history, then one might expect it to receive the same handling as any other vital subject: analytical and dispassionate. Furthermore, a study of totalitarianism as an abstraction has greater potential for making today's real world comprehensible to adolescents than does the more common treatment of individual Communist states. While it is the military threat posed by Communist nations that has most alarmed Americans and led to their insistence that communism be studied in the schools, it is the more subtle and complex attack of totalitarian ideas and approaches on our democratic institutions that deserves primary attention.

Concentrating on the concept—totalitarianism—rather than studying the many forms it has taken also enables a student to have a better picture of his own system. If he views communism as the only threat to democracy, he may ignore or even welcome the assistance of equally totalitarian groups that draw support by being vigorously anti-communist. A study of totalitarianism and its cost to the individual should also contribute to a healthier and more sensitive understanding of democratic systems.

NOTE ON THE USE OF THIS GUIDE

The purpose of this guide is to acquaint teachers with certain basic generalizations related to the concept of totalitarianism and to suggest ways in which these generalizations may be introduced inductively to students. Although the guide attempts to clarify each generalization it introduces, it cannot pretend to provide complete information about the history and development of totalitarianism or give a full description of the various forms it has taken. Quite the contrary! This guide was originally conceived as a supplement and complement to the booklet by William Ebenstein, *Totalitarianism: New Perspectives* (New York: Holt, Rinehart, and Winston, Inc., 1962).[1] Ebenstein's booklet and this guide may be viewed as two parts of a teachers' resource unit with Ebenstein providing the content and this guide the application of the content.

The generalizations posed in this guide constitute pieces of a jig-saw puzzle: when put together, they make possible some modest understanding of totalitarianism as a concept. This concept or abstraction can then be used to judge individual nation-states that are the subject of future or on-going study. This approach is designed to endow the student with an understanding of totalitarianism which, in form, resembles the kind of understanding of democracy he achieves—hopefully—after studying a variety of democratic systems. Just as British and American governments differ greatly in form but coincide in their commitment to the democratic principle, so do such disparate totalitarian gov-

---

[1] References to Ebenstein throughout this guide pertain to this booklet.

ernments as Nazi Germany and Communist China resemble each other in their methods of control. In teaching about democracy, teachers now avoid an over-reliance on the American example, for such a procedure can create the impression that democracy finds its only embodiment in the American form of government. Similarly, when teaching about totalitarianism, teachers need to avoid an over-emphasis on the Soviet system, a tendency which not only implies a false equation of totalitarianism and Russian government but also excludes other, equally totalitarian states. One of the tasks of this guide, therefore, is to suggest generalizations which characterize all totalitarian systems in varying degrees and which, when fully understood, may be used as tools for the analyses of specific political units.

Clearly, many opportunities already exist for introducing one or more of these generalizations in the usual content of present social studies courses. A world history course, for example, offers occasions for describing Nazi Germany, Fascist Italy, pre-World War II Japan, Castro's Cuba, Peron's Argentina, and Trujillo's Dominican Republic. One may also suggest elements of totalitarianism when describing life in ancient Sparta, apartheid in South Africa, and the "know-nothings" and the Ku Klux Klan in the United States. However desirable a mention of totalitarianism at a variety of points in the school's social studies curriculum might be, this is inevitably a hit-or-miss approach, which generally denies the student the opportunity to weave all the bits and pieces into a meaningful concept.

With the assumption that there is ample justification to teach the concept of totalitarianism as a unit in and of itself, this guide seeks to present material and instructional aids for a distinct unit of study. Such a unit might be a portion of Problems of Democracy, World History, American History, American Government, or other courses now offered in high school social studies. The most appropriate place for the unit can best be decided by the individual school's faculty and administration.

Since the purpose of this guide is to provide a complete teaching unit which may be used as it stands, books, visual aids, and other resources are mentioned only when they contribute to the specific purposes of the unit. There has been no attempt to list all the materials that exist on the subject of totalitarianism and which might be useful to a teacher designing his own unit. Many teachers will doubtless want to use additional materials in conjunction with this unit.

The unit is constructed around inductive principles of teaching. Much has been written about the importance of using inductive approaches to the teaching of social studies, but little has appeared in a form which teachers can use. This guide represents an attempt to teach inductively to high school students a complex abstraction drawn from the social sciences. Any success that it enjoys will depend largely upon the teacher's understanding of the inductive process and the intentions of the unit.

Each teacher must, first of all, understand clearly the meaning of the term *concept*. A concept is an idea that includes all that is associated with or suggested by a term. Totalitarianism may be defined rather simply as a political, social, and economic phenomenon which seeks the total subjection of the individual to the state. While essentially accurate, such a definition may be meaningless to the student who has little knowledge about what "total subjection of the individual" could mean. To the person who has read widely about totalitarianism or has experienced its effects himself, the term may evoke—among other things—the knock on the door late at night; the closing of churches; religious, ethnic, or racial persecution; blind devotion to a set of political ideas proclaimed by a leader; war; and economic sacrifice to advance the aspirations of political leaders. Such a person can *conceptualize* the abstraction while the student can only *define* it.

This unit is designed to assist students in reaching a sophisticated level of conceptualization. Rather than introducing him to the term and requiring him to define it, the unit sets forth a series of generalizations about totalitarianism so that the student may fashion his own conception of totalitarianism. These generalizations are analogous to building blocks. When the edifice has been constructed, the student should be able to stand back from it and define what he has built; but his definition should have far greater meaning for him than it would have had in the beginning.

In addition, each generalization is presented inductively insofar as possible. The teacher is given an activity, a reading, or some visual aid to use in class. Questions are provided which should lead the student to arrive at the generalization on his own. Having "discovered" the generalization for himself, the student is more likely to understand it and to retain it than if he were asked only to memorize what a teacher has told him.

There always exists the question of how much a student should know before he can generalize with reasonable accuracy. Some scholars would insist that a student who wishes to understand totalitarianism must have studied a great deal of history and political philosophy. While it is difficult to refute this argument, since it places one in the position of arguing that a little knowledge is as useful as considerable knowledge, it is clear that we cannot wait until students have completed graduate school before introducing them to major concepts. If Jerome Bruner and others are correct, meaningful concepts can be introduced with intellectual honesty at any age—provided they are introduced in a way befitting the maturity and experience of the students. The unit which follows is based on the assumption that one need not know everything about Nazi Germany or Soviet Rusisa to understand totalitarianism, but that a limited amount of information used honestly and wisely can lay the basis for an understanding of a sophisticated concept. While generalizing too soon on too limited informaton is indeed dangerous, it may be equally disastrous to refuse to permit students to generalize at all until they know everything about a topic.

Finally, while the guide constitutes a complete unit in itself, it would be futile and undesirable to expect all teachers to use it in the same way. Much depends upon the unique talent and style of the teacher, the number of days that have been set aside for teaching the unit, the ability of the students, other sources of information available to the teacher, and the environment of the school and community. All of these must be considered by the teacher so that the unit can be adjusted accordingly. The success of the unit thus depends not so much upon the pages that follow as upon the ability of the teacher to translate them into a meaningful experience for his students.

CHAPTER II

Facets of Totalitarianism: Nine Generalizations

Generalization No. 1

The nature of the political system which will evolve in any nation depends in part upon the values held by its citizens.

What is a good political system? What is good government? To a considerable extent, the responses to these questions depend upon one's values. If a person prizes efficiency above everything else, he will admire the government that "gets things done," regardless of the method it uses. If one agrees with two former American political leaders that what is good for General Motors is good for the United States, or that the business of the United States is business, then a clear test of good government for him would be the health of the business community. If a person believes, as did Thomas Jefferson, "that government is best which governs least," he will want a government which makes itself inconspicuous. On the other hand, if one believes that the primary task of government is to advance the physical, moral, and spiritual well-being of all its citizens by direct intervention, such a person might well accept activities by government which would be anathemas to those who believe that such activities are best left to individuals.

Students should learn that what we judge to be right and proper depends upon our values. Many of the most commonly held and accepted values in a society are never discussed, precisely because they are taken for granted. It is when values come to be questioned that they are subjected to overt scrutiny and discussion. The deepest values of a society in some ways resemble the earth's atmosphere, almost invisible, all-pervading, important to life, and largely ignored except when the air is disturbed or the weather is inclement. Yet the combination of elements around a planet determines the absence or presence of life; the nature of those elements affects the nature of existence.

As students go through the activities suggested at the end of this section, they should be encouraged to consider the obvious and everyday, as well as the exotic or controversial, values of a society.

In beginning a study of totalitarianism, students might try to assume the attitude a cultural anthropologist takes when he approaches a society. In order to be as objective and clear as possible, a student must understand the values which guide his own life as he discovers the values which direct the actions of those he is observing. Because values represent dominant forces in all political systems and in all societies, students should attempt through dispassionate analysis to understand *why*, in addition to *how*, individuals behave as they do in societies.

For the purposes of this lesson, it is useful to lead students through three steps: A definition of values, a brief examination of widely held American values, and a discovery of some values that have directed totalitarian states.

What does the term "values" mean when used in a cultural sense? Values are ideas which are cherished or prized by a given group of people. As cherished ideas, they tend to set standards for acceptable behavior and to establish norms for judging the good life. Values are beliefs which serve to inspire people to act in socially desirable ways. Values may be uncovered in the ethical code of a society and in the formal laws which control the actions of its citizens. Values may be enforced by parental reproof, by social ostracism, or by the full power of the state acting as the guardian of the social code.

There are hierarchies of values. Some values reflect a consensus of the American people; some are regional; others are related to occupations, social class, and religious and ethnic origins. Some values are guarded by the power of the state—an opposition to cannibalism; some are fostered by private associations—temperance or abstinence in the use of alcoholic beverages; others are observed by individuals acting alone—showing disgust to loud belching in public. In each of the above instances, questions of values are at stake. Some are judged to be issues of major importance; others are considered to be less serious but potential sources of minor frictions and displeasure.

Values are not inherited; they must be learned. And every society, with varying degrees of awareness and sophistication, considers the task of transmitting its values to the coming generations —through public institutions, such as schools, and through the ubiquitous institution, the family—to be one of its primary functions. Cultural anthropologists have shown that values are quite different in various parts of the world, that there are no absolute values. Values are created by factors of environment and historical experience. Thus, what seems necessary to one society may seem ridiculous to another. Even within a society—especially one which we call modern—values are constantly undergoing examination and revision. What seems right and proper in one age will not seem so to later generations. One need only recall the changing role and status of women in American society during the last 75 years. Also, values may differ within a nation at any one point in time. In the United States, there are perceptible regional differences: north and south; east, midwest and west; rural and urban. Nevertheless, it is possible to speak of American values which seem to reflect a consensus of American belief. Some examples are the right of each individual to seek any position in life to which his ambition and talent may entitle him; the idea that governments exist to serve man, not vice versa; and the fact that individual and institutional power is governed by constitutional law rather than by the arbitrary decisions of a ruling elite.

Often our values conflict with each other. We want the police to be vigorous in stamping out organized crime, yet we might hamper their actions by our refusal to permit wiretapping or the conducting of searches without proper warrants. We may value the right of each individual to seek work without discrimination because of race or religion, and simultaneously resist legal measures which would take away an employer's right to hire the people he wants. In such instances one value gives way to another, or we seek to find a point of agreement between the values in conflict.

Consciously or unconsciously, values are frequently assigned priorities or given different weights.

Emergencies may also force a nation to sacrifice—at least temporarily—certain long-held values for others. Few ideas are so cherished in the United States as the right of Americans to live where they choose and the belief that the price of goods should be fixed by the market place, not by government. Yet in World War II, both values were supplanted by the values of efficiency and security in winning the war. The Nisei—Japanese-Americans living on the west coast—were forced to relocate in Colorado and other less-sensitive areas of the country because of the fear that they were a potential source of sabotage and treason. Similarly, war conditions led the government to ration goods and to fix prices in order to prevent rampant inflation and to provide a more equitable distribution of scarce goods. Another important value is the right of men to speak freely, yet from the time of the Alien and Sedition Acts this value has been seriously questioned during periods of national crisis.

Suggested Procedure

Through class discussion you can help students arrive at an acceptable definition of "value." Then the class might be asked to list what they believe to be basic American values. As these are contributed and agreed to by the class, they may be written on the board by the teacher and in their notebooks by the students. Teachers who wish references for this phase of the activity, either as background for themselves or as reading material for their students, will find the following sources especially useful: one is a pamphlet by Ralph Gabriel[2] in which he discusses what seems to him to be basic American values, a second is *Goals for Americans*,[3] which states implicitly values embraced by most Americans, and the third is *The Power of the Democratic Idea*,[4]

[2] Ralph H. Gabriel, *Traditional Values in American Life*. New York: Harcourt, Brace and World, Inc. and UNESCO, 1963.
[3] *Goals for Americans: The Report of the President's Commission on National Goals*. New York: The American Assembly and Prentice-Hall, Inc., 1960.
[4] *The Power of the Democratic Idea: Report VI, Prospect for America*. Garden City, N.Y.: Rockefeller Brothers Fund and Doubleday and Company, Inc., 1960.

which is Report VI of *Prospect for America*. Each of these book-lets examines the American political and social tradition, and the authors express in terms which students can understand values that are held uppermost in the minds of most Americans. Although high school students are unlikely to reach a final and complete listing of American values, some effort to identify these in the beginning of this study will prove useful as students become more deeply involved in the study of non-democratic countries.

The political leaders of totalitarian societies are also motivated by values. Like our own, the values they hold are conditioned by their environments and historical experiences. The scope of this booklet does not permit a detailed description of the historical and environmental conditions that have led each totalitarian society to adopt its own particular political pattern. Such a study is indeed important, and teachers may wish to include it with their own study of totalitarianism. Nevertheless, it is sufficient for the purpose of this guide to recognize that totalitarian systems have values and to identify some of the values that have commanded their energies.

The following quotes taken from the speeches and writings of leaders of totalitarian movements contain clues as to the specific values held by totalitarians. No attempt has been made to include all the values embraced by a specific totalitarian society, nor has there been an effort to include examples from all totalitarian societies. These statements merely give students an opportunity to pick out some of the values which have stimulated totalitarian leaders and their followers. Students can identify these values and compare them to the list of American values previously identified in class.

The following statements may be mimeographed and distributed to students to read at their desks, or they may be prepared to use with the overhead projector. In either case, students should be asked to read the quotation and then decide what value or values it implicitly or explicitly contains. After the students have identified the values reflected in the quotations and compared them to the list of American values they had listed earlier, the class might speculate on the types of programs and policies that could emerge if a society adopted and acted upon the values stated by the leaders of totalitarian states. Perceptive students are likely to describe activities which have actually taken place in states such as Fascist Italy, Nazi Germany, Soviet Russia, and Communist China. The ability to predict the consequences of one's values is a skill that is important to develop in high school students.

VALUE STATEMENTS OF TOTALITARIAN LEADERS

Benito Mussolini:

" 'For Fascism, the State is not the night-watchman who is concerned only with the personal security of the citizens; nor is it an organization for purely material ends, such as that of guaranteeing a certain degree of prosperity and a relatively peaceful social order, to achieve which a council of administration would be sufficient, nor is it a creation of mere politics with no contact with the material and complex reality of the lives of individuals and the life of peoples. The State, as conceived by Fascism and as it acts, is a spiritual and moral fact because it makes concrete the political, juridical, economic organization of the nation and such an organization is, in its origin and in its development, a manifestation of the spirit. The State is the guarantor of internal and external security, but it is also the guardian and the transmitter of the spirit of the people as it has been elaborated through the centuries in language, custom, faith. The State is not only present, it is also past, and above all future. It is the State which, transcending the brief limit of individual lives, represents the immanent conscience of the nation. The forms in which States express themselves change, but the necessity of the State remains. It is the State which educates citizens for civic virtue, makes them conscious of their mission, calls them to unity; harmonizes their interests in justice; hands on the achievements of thought in the sciences, the arts, in law, in human solidarity; it carries men from the elementary life of the tribe to the highest human expression of power which is Empire; it entrusts to the ages the names of those who died for its integrity or in obedience to its laws; it puts forward as an example and recommends to the generations that are to come the leaders who increased its territory and the men of genius who gave it glory. When the sense of the State declines and the disintegrating and centrifugal tendencies of individuals and groups prevail, national societies move to their decline.' "[5]

Adolf Hitler:

"The will to live leads beyond the limitations of the present to the struggle for the prerequisites of life. Struggle is the impulse of self-preservation in nature. Man has become great through struggle.

"The first fundamental of any rational *Weltanschauung* [world outlook] is the fact that on earth and in the universe force alone is decisive. Whatever goal man has reached is due to his originality plus his brutality. Whatever man possesses today in the field of culture is the culture of the Aryan race. The Aryan has stamped his character on the whole world. The basis for all development is the creative urge of the individual, not the vote of majorities. The genius of the individual is decisive, not the spirit of the masses. All life is bound up in three theses: Struggle is the father of all things, virtue lies in blood, leadership is primary and decisive.

"Because the German people has forgotten this, it has collapsed. And if the German people does not again acquire power, that is, power in the sense of values and will, then no other choice is left the German people but to perish. There will never be a solution of the German problem until we return to the three fundamental principles which control the existence of every nation: The concept of struggle, the purity of blood, and the ingenuity of the individual."[6]

Josef Stalin:

"It is sometimes asked whether it is not possible to slow down the tempo somewhat, to put a check on the movement. No, com-

[5] Benito Mussolini, *The Doctrines of Fascism;* reprinted in *The Social and Political Doctrines of Contemporary Europe,* ed. by Michael Oakeshott. New York: Cambridge University Press, 1942, p. 176.

[6] Adolph Hitler, "Speech at Chemnitz, April 2, 1928"; *Volkisches Beobachter,* April 7, 1928; reprinted in *Communism, Fascism, and Democracy: The Theoretical Foundations,* ed. by Carl Cohen. New York: Random House, 1963, p. 409.

rades, it is not possible! The tempo must not be reduced! On the contrary, we must increase it as much as is within our powers and possibilities. . . .

"To slacken the tempo would mean falling behind. And those who fall behind get beaten. But we do not want to be beaten. No, we refuse to be beaten! One feature of the history of old Russia was the continual beatings she suffered because of her backwardness. She was beaten by the Mongol khans. She was beaten by the Turkish beys. She was beaten by the Swedish feudal lords. She was beaten by the Polish and Lithuanian gentry. She was beaten by the British and French capitalists. She was beaten by the Japanese barons. All beat her—because of her backwardness, because of her military backwardness, cultural backwardness, political backwardness, industrial backwardness, agricultural backwardness. They beat her because to do so was profitable and could be done with impunity. . . . Such is the law of the exploiters—to beat the backward and the weak. It is the jungle law of capitalism. You are backward, you are weak—therefore, you are wrong; hence, you can be beaten and enslaved. You are mighty—therefore you are right; hence, we must be wary of you.

"That is why we must no longer lag behind.

"In the past we had no fatherland, nor could we have had one. But now that we have overthrown capitalism and power is in our hands, in the hands of the people, we have a fatherland, and we will uphold its independence. Do you want our socialist fatherland to be beaten and to lose its independence? If you do not want this, you must put an end to its backwardness in the shortest possible time and develop genuine Bolshevik tempo in building up its socialist economy. There is no other way. That is why Lenin said on the eve of the October Revolution: 'Either perish, or overtake and outstrip the advanced capitalist countries.'

"We are fifty or a hundred years behind the advanced countries. We must make good this distance in ten years. Either we do it, or we shall go under."[7]

---

[7] Josef Stalin, "The Tasks of Business Executives." Speech Delivered at the First All-Union Conference of Leading Personnel of Socialist Industry, February 4, 1931, from *J. V. Stalin: Works*, Volume 13. Moscow: Foreign Languages Publishing House, 1955, pp. 40-41.

Mao Tse-tung:

"The purpose of our meeting today is precisely to fit art and literature properly into the whole revolutionary machine as one of its component parts, to make them a powerful weapon for uniting and educating the people and for attacking and annihilating the enemy, and to help the people to fight the enemy with one heart and one mind. . . .

"In the world today all culture, all art and literature belong to definite classes and follow definite political lines. There is in reality no such thing as art for art's sake, art which stands above classes or art which runs parallel to or remains independent of politics. Proletarian art and literature are part of the entire cause of the proletarian revolution, in the words of Lenin, 'cogs and screws in the whole machine.' Therefore the Party's artistic and literary activity occupies a definite and assigned position in the Party's total revolutionary work and is subordinated to the prescribed revolutionary task of the Party in a given revolutionary period. . . . Art and literature are subordinate to politics, but they in turn also exert a great influence on politics."[8]

---

[8] Mao Tse-tung, "Talks at the Yenan Forum on Art and Literature," May 2 and 23, 1942. *Mao Tse-tung: Selected Works*, Volume 4. New York: International Publishers, 1956, pp. 64; 82. By pemission of International Publishers Co., Inc.

OUTLINE OF LESSON PLAN

Through class discussion students arrive at a definition of the term "value."

Students suggest a list of basic American values which are listed on the board by the teacher and in their notebooks by the students.

Teacher distributes mimeographed copies of quotations by totalitarian leaders. Students pick out the values implict in the passages.

Students speculate about the possible consequences of such values and compare the values of totalitarian leaders with the list of basic American values previously agreed upon by the class.

Estimated time required for this lesson: one or two class periods

---

Generalization No. 2

All societies cope with the problem of individual freedom versus public control. No contemporary society can be judged to be either completely free or completely totalitarian. Nevertheless, nations differ markedly and significantly in their attitudes toward and treatment of the relationship between freedom and control; these differences form identifiable but rather loosely defined and fluctuating patterns.

It is important to make clear to students early in their study of totalitarianism that no actual state fits exactly the model of a totalitarian state, just as no democratic state measures up to the ideal of a free and open society. Comparing democracy and totalitarianism is not contrasting black with white but distinguishing among discrete areas of a spectrum. Although the differences in the shades may be quite significant in some cases, students must understand that *all* societies grapple with the problems of individual autonomy and public control. Who decides how power shall be divided between the individual and the state, and the techniques used to maintain primary control by one or the other give us clues to the nature of that society.

Individual states are by no means consistent within themselves. Greater control is exercised in some spheres of public life than in others. Moreover, conditions both at home and abroad may trigger new responses within a nation. During times of national peril the government of a democratic state may extend its control to many private areas of life, and exert new types of control, even adopting techniques of totalitarian systems. A period of international peace and domestic tranquillity, on the other hand, may encourage totalitarian rulers to relax many of their controls. Societies and government are never static, never completely fixed in one mold.

In addition to understanding the complexity of categorizing societies in motion, students must also appreciate the inherent problems of model building. Models are useful for analytical purposes as they approximate the real world. Nevertheless, models can never replicate the real world. The model remains an abstraction, a framework, a tool for analysis. Real states do not conform to the precise dimensions of even the most brilliantly conceived model. Models can and do serve scholars, however, by helping them classify phenomena in the real world.

In this lesson students are encouraged to begin building their own models of totalitarianism by examining the various ways in which societies organize basic activities. The way everyday life is regulated indicates the degree of control which the community at large or political elites may exert over individuals within societies. The more in the direction of totalitarianism a society moves, the less freedom remains for the individual to do as he chooses. The more free and open a society becomes, the more opportunities exist for the individual to follow his own dictates.

This lesson will help students consider three major ideas: (1) There are real differences in the degree of freedom available to citizens in different societies participating in the same basic social activities; (2) these differences—though significant—are generally matters of degree rather than polar opposites; and (3) nations are rarely frozen in one position along the continuum which ranges from freedom to control.

The line graph which follows can be used to convey these ideas to students. The extremes on the graph indicate total autonomy and total control. The graph and the questions which accompany it may be duplicated so that students can have copies at their desks.

> Note: The statements are grouped by topic for purposes of comparison. They are *not* ranked within the topic according to degrees of control. This prevents the student from simply ranking them as listed. The statements are worded hypothetically, but they are based upon actual conditions. Specific names have been omitted so that students will not rank the statements according to the stereotypes or particular images they have of individual countries.
>
> See pages 21-23 for suggested ways of using the graph in class.

INTRODUCTION

People engage in similar social activities, but the freedom with which they lead their everyday lives varies from society to society, from nation to nation. The line graph below contains points between two extremes—complete freedom or autonomy at one end, total control of the individual at the other.

Work:

_____11. An individual can work wherever his talent and skill permits.

_____12. An individual cannot quit unless his employer grants him permission to do so.

_____13. An individual may work only if he agrees to join an association of other workers.

_____14. The individual must work where his talent and skill are most desired by society.

_____15. Citizens who are either unwilling or unable to work are supported by society.

Education:

_____16. Education for all children is compulsory.

_____17. Education is free to all who desire it.

_____18. The individual is free to choose an education most befitting his career goals.

_____19. The school curriculum and standards of performance are determined by the national government.

_____20. The schools reflect the values and interests of the local community.

Individual Expression:

_____21. The state censors those examples of art and literature that are viewed as immoral or distasteful to the public.

_____22. The individual is free to express himself in whatever manner he chooses.

_____23. The individual can say what he wants so long as he does not endanger the freedom of others.

_____24. A person can criticize his political leaders.

_____25. All forms of mass communication are controlled by the state and subject to its will.

Relationship between State and the Individual:

_____26. The state is viewed as the servant of its citizens.

_____27. The individual exists primarily to advance the interest of all of society.

_____28. Society can demand the property and even the lives of its citizens.

_____29. Certain ethnic, racial, or religious groups are imprisoned because they are deemed to be dangerous to the state.

_____30. An individual may not travel or move his residence without permission of the government.

DIRECTIONS

On the blank preceding each statement, place the
which corresponds to the position the statement should
the line graph. For example, if you believe that Statemer
ber One represents almost total control of the individua
"5" or "6" in front of the statement. The other numbers
lesser degrees of control. As you read each statement dc
to decide what contemporary nation-state conforms to t
ment. Simply ask yourself these questions: "What te
would a society have if it behaved in this manner? Wor
in the direction of one or in the direction of six? Ho
either direction?" You may wish to compare the stateme
in each category.

Graph #1

(A society in which the
individual is free of
external control)

(A society
individua
controlled
sources of

1	2	3	4	5

Marriage and Family:

_____ 1. People are not bound by any marriage laws or
_____ 2. People are prevented by social pressure from mar
of a different racial, ethnic, or religious group.
_____ 3. A license and a blood test are required before a
marry.
_____ 4. To improve the physical and mental qualities of
people are prevented from marrying physical or
fectives unless the man or woman agrees to ste
_____ 5. The family chooses the spouse for its son or dau

Belief:

_____ 6. All citizens must believe in and adhere to one sε
_____ 7. All beliefs—even non-belief—are practiced.
_____ 8. A person who holds unpopular beliefs may lose
be investigated by the government.
_____ 9. Citizens are free to challenge widely held belie
_____10. A person is not permitted to practice a belief tl
the health or security of society.

SUGGESTED PROCEDURE

There are at least two ways to begin this lesson. You might distribute the statements to the entire class and allow from 20 to 30 minutes for the students to classify each of the statements. You should indicate that there are no final responses to these statements and that students should treat each statement as an abstraction, *not* as a specific manifestation of a contemporary nation-state. If left uninstructed, some students will decide that the United States is two or three and the Soviet Union is six. Then they will simply number the statements according to whether the characteristics are found in the United States or the Soviet Union, thereby avoiding decisions on the statements as they might apply to societies in general. When the class has finished numbering the statements, you might ask individual students to read their answers and see if it is possible for the class to reach a consensus on categorizing each of the statements.

Another way to proceed is to divide the class into six discussion groups. After the statements have been distributed to the students, assign each of the discussion groups one category to prepare for a group report to the class. This means that if group one has been assigned *Marriage and Family*, this group must reach a consensus on statements one through five; the discussion leader will present the group view to the class. This approach requires students to discuss thoroughly the five statements under one category in order to reach a consensus. You should allow 15 to 20 minutes for the group discussion before calling for the reports. Suggest to the class that they consider the group decision a decision for all unless there is strong opposition to a number assigned to any of the statements. When such opposition appears, permit the dissent to be heard and be ready to begin a search for a new consensus.

The class activities described above are certain to require at least one class period. As homework for the following day, ask students to prepare six captions under which they can group all the statements that have identical numbers. For example, students should suggest a label which characterizes all the statements marked as one, a label that fits all statements marked two, etc. Students should not use the names of nations but rather descriptive adjectives or nouns, e.g., dictatorship, utopia, anarchy, etc. In class on the following day, ask individuals to contribute their suggestions for captions and to explain what the captions mean to them: For example, if a student suggests "anarchy" for all statements with number one in the blanks, does he mean chaos or absence of government? Class time may be used to harmonize divergent suggestions into a set of categories which seems reasonable and workable to the class as a whole. The students' categories might look like the following:

(1)	(2)	(3)	(4)	(5)	(6)
Anarchy	Ideal Democratic Society	Contemporary Democratic Societies	Democratic Society Undergoing Crisis, e.g., War, Depression	Dictatorship	Model of the Totalitarian Society

While such categories are no more precise than the statements they presume to cover, such an analysis does make clear to students that the relationship between the individual and the state is not fixed but may vary as political, economic, and social conditions change.

During wartime, democratic governments usually impose controls and restrictions which closely resemble those used in totalitarian states. For example, statement No. 29 will remind students of concentration camps in Nazi Germany and the USSR, but it can also apply to camps established during World War II for Japanese-Americans. While the conditions of the camps for Japanese-Americans in the United States bear little resemblance to those at Dachau, Belsen, and Buchenwald, the treatment of Nisei and the abruptness and thoroughness with which they were denied freedom of movement during the war did reflect a drift toward totalitarianism in this country.[9]

After having used the scale and developed and refined a set of categories, students should write down or state in their own

---

[9] If you wish to make this point even more forceful to your students, you might show them a film from the Twentieth Century television series, "The Nisei: The Pride and the Shame" which is available from the Prudential Insurance Company. This film makes obvious the breakdown of civil liberties in the United States as a result of war-time pressures.

words the main point of this lesson. By emphasizing the complexity of the dynamic between freedom and authority, you can lead students to state the generalizations which were the subject of this lesson. You might also find it useful to relate this lesson to the previous lesson on values.

OUTLINE OF LESSON PLAN

Graph #1 (p. 18-20) is given to the students.

Rating procedures are explained.

Students rate statements on individual copies. The class may be divided into six committees. Each of the committees would rate one section.

Individual or committee ratings are presented to the class.

Class discussion to reach consensus on ratings.

Homework assignment is for students to prepare a series of categories under which they can list the statements.

Students report their suggestions to the class, and the class strives to reach an agreement on the categories.

Students formulate Generalization 2 in their own words.

Estimated time required for this lesson: two or three class periods

---

Generalization No. 3

Totalitarian regimes depend upon a command mechanism to run their economic systems.

This lesson is designed to help students understand the nature of a totalitarian economy. Just as the leaders of totalitarian societies control political and social aspects of life, so do they exert major control over economic activities. The over-riding fact to keep in mind is that their control is planned and purposeful; all segments of the society are directed toward the achievement of primary goals set forth by the leaders. It does not matter whether the goal is to preserve peace, to make war, to industrialize, or to build windmills—all private aspirations and economic activities are subordinated to the expressed and public objectives of the state.

Although this lesson is not intended to teach students economics and, in fact, assumes a certain level of economic understanding, it might be useful to review some current theories and insights.

The study of economics is an examination of how a society tries to resolve the problem of limited resources and unlimited wants. The fact of scarcity—there are not enough resources to satisfy all human desires—requires a society to make continuous choices. A society must decide what to produce, how to produce the chosen goods and services, and how to distribute the fruits of production among its members. Steel used to produce automobiles cannot be used to build railroads, buildings, or factories and tools to make more steel. The decision to make automobiles is also a decision *not* to produce other things which require steel. Similarly, the decision to grow peanuts one year is a decision not to produce cotton from a particular acreage.

Various institutions which provide guidelines for making economic decisions have evolved. In *The Making of Economic Society*, Robert L. Heilbroner classifies these institutions according to three general systems or patterns of economic decision-making: tradition, command, and market. An economy run by tradition is one in which basic economic questions are decided by the forces of custom and the immediate environment. In traditional societies, children usually grow up to assume the job or trade of their fathers, and they are expected to perform their tasks, e.g., farming or hunting, or their trades, such as carpentry, exactly as their fathers did. The emphasis is upon preserving the *status quo* rather than upon promoting change. Although traditional societies are largely self-sufficient economically, their dependence upon skills and a fortuitous mother nature, and their rigidity render them helpless in the face of natural disasters and profound technological change.

An economic system may also be organized according to "command." A command economy is one in which the basic economic questions are answered by an elite. The decision-making elite may consist of an individual, such as a Roman emperor; a group, such as a political party in Communist China or Nazi Germany; or a democratically elected government. The objectives of the

command economy vary according to the objectives of the decision-making body. The Roman emperor might simply order struc-
tures built in his honor; the group governs economic activities
within the framework of its political views; a democratically
elected government might carry out only those functions, e.g.,
road-building or national defense, which private segments of the
society cannot manage.

A third type of economic system is the "market." The system
run by the market is the most difficult of all to describe, because
its dynamism depends on a multitude of factors. The market approach leaves basic economic decisions up to individuals. *What*
will be produced is what people demand. *How* goods and services are produced depends on the efficiency and skill of individuals to produce goods for consumers at prices which they are
willing to pay. Run by the desires of the consumers and the lure
of profits and wages for manufacturers and workers, a circular
mechanism evolves: Increased competition which leads to spe-
cialization, imaginative management, and optimum use of resources, tends to drive down prices. Those who cannot compete
are forced into other avenues of the economy, or are driven to
create new avenues. Workers go where they can earn the highest
rewards for their given skills. The wages they receive determine
their standard of living, their roles as consumers, the quality and
quantity of goods and services they purchase from the manufacturers. Both employers and employees are simultaneously pro-
ducers and consumers.

In reality, no modern economic system adopts one of the three
approaches at the exclusion of all the others. The American boy
who decides to stay on the farm with his father probably made
his choice on the basis of custom. If he had first surveyed career
opportunities and decided to become a doctor because doctors
seemed to receive more income and prestige than farmers, his
decision would have been prompted by market incentives. If, on
the other hand, regardless of his personal preferences, he finds
that he must serve two years in the army because the local draft
board selected him for this task, the decision about what he will
do is not his but a result of command.

Tradition, command, and market all are represented in the

American economic system; but in normal circumstances we have come to rely on the market to make most of our economic decisions. The key lies in the phrase *in normal circumstances*, for when times have not been "normal," Americans have permitted their government to exercise extensive control over economic activities. During World War II, the United States government made many decisions about *what* to produce: Tanks and military vehicles replaced automobiles on the assembly lines. The government decided *how* to produce goods, how to use human and material resources. Our government also determined patterns of distribution. Price control and rationing were only two of the ways in which command mechanisms took over the normal functions of the price system to distribute the relatively few goods produced for domestic use.

Totalitarian systems inevitably adopt command mechanisms to order the lives of their nations. Totalitarian systems are either created by emergencies, or they create their own emergencies. Therefore, the full resources of society must constanty be mobilized to meet crises as they are determined by political leaders. A "crisis" may be the urgent desire to catch up with other countries economically or the need to prepare for war, either aggressively or to repel impending invasion.

Command approaches may be grafted onto capitalist or traditional bases. In those Communist societies which have come into being by internal revolution, command has been imposed upon a traditional, peasant society in order to force rapid industrialization and economic development. To achieve industrialization and growth as quickly as possible, the five-year plans which Stalin instituted in 1929 promoted enforced collectivization of agriculture, destruction of union power, and many other expedients of the command system. The Soviet experiments in economic development and the techniques used to transform a backward economy into a modern, industrial system are highly attractive to many underdeveloped societies.

Command has also been added to theretofore market societies. In Nazi Germany, Fascist Italy, and Imperial Japan, most economic decisions were made on the basis of such considerations as profit, competition, and consumer wants and needs. Nevertheless, mobilization for war caused by imperialist ambitions required a careful allocation of resources, and led these nations to adopt mechanisms which in purpose and detail were the same as those used in Soviet Russia. Those factory owners in Nazi Germany who retained title to their plants had little to say about what they would produce or the wages they would pay their workers. All aspects of production, distribution, and compensation were determined by the state.

Just as tradition, command, and market are all represented in the American system, so too can the three approaches be found in totalitarian societies. In the USSR, consumers decide what they will buy from the goods produced at the command of the state. Bonuses spur both workers and managers to greater efficiency. Peasants may still supplement their incomes by selling products grown in their own garden plots. These examples reflect the market at work in the Soviet Union. Nevertheless, the elements of command predominate in Communist societies, and the forces of the market govern the United States economy. If we were to display a continuum, it might look something like this:

```
pure market                                    pure command
economy                                             economy
        U.S.                            U.S.S.R.
|_____^_____^_____|
```

In a study of command economic systems, it is important to consider the quality or kind of command, as well as the degree of command that exists in the society. Americans grumbled about but tolerated the restrictions brought on by World War II, because economic decisions were made by a government elected by and responsible to the will of the people. As director of the OPA, Chester Bowles wrote: "We will continue to get plenty of criticism, and as long as it's constructive criticism, we'll welcome it and try to learn from it. Our country's editorial writers, commentators and columnists not only have the right but the obligation to point out the weak spots in our government and demand that those weaknesses be corrected. It is the job of Congress, as the elected representatives of the people to keep a sharp eye on Government budget, and Government procedures, and

Government personnel and activities. This Congressional watchfulness and control is an essential part of our American system. It must continue if we are to maintain our democracy. . . . I have said that the OPA was created to control rents and the cost of living, to spread the supply of scarce products in the fairest possible way among all our citizens, and to maintain a stable economy on which to build a postwar world which will provide economic security and true freedom for every American citizen." (*Life*, December 13, 1943, p. 64.)

Most Americans accepted the controls as necessary to winning the war, and they took it for granted that once the war ended, they would again be free to buy and sell, eat and drink, and work and play as they pleased. Such is not the case in totalitarian states. There, political leaders determine the duration and seriousness of the "emergency," as well as the sacrifices needed to survive it. Individual citizens have no confidence that they shall ever have a real hand in making economic decisions. However, many citizens in totalitarian states do have the confidence that they are participating in and contributing to goals which transcend their individual desires.

As we have mentioned, the goals of a command economy vary according to the objectives of the political leaders, but every totalitarian system always has expressed goals. Both long-range and immediate goals are used by the decision-making elite to implement and to justify all aspects of the command economy.

Suggested Procedure

This lesson will probably require two days. On the first day, you might review basic principles of economics with your students, covering essentially the points raised in the introduction to this lesson: What economic questions must be faced by all societies? What are the principal characteristics and essential ingredients of tradition, command, and market systems? If the students have previously studied economics, such a review can be accomplished in one class period. If they are not familiar with basic economic principles, you might have to set aside more time for this phase of the lesson.

The point of this lesson is to show students why totalitarian systems adopt command mechanisms. A selection from *Animal Farm* was chosen because it demonstrates the idea of the lesson simply and directly without getting a student lost in the economic details of a modern totalitarian state; and the use of a fantasy requires a kind of analysis not required by the reading of a direct description of a real economic system. As students read the selection for class discussion, they should pay close attention to the questions which precede the reading.

During the class discussion students might consider the following questions:

1. Look at the line graph in Generalization No. 2. Where would you place *Animal Farm* on the spectrum? Why?
2. Compare what you know about Napoleon with the value statements of totalitarian leaders in Generalization No. 1. Do any of those quotations seem to be similar to the values Napoleon must have held? (See Stalin's statement.)
3. Why did Napoleon decide to build a windmill? Were his reasons the same as those of the other animals? Were Napoleon's reasons the same as Snowball's?
4. What other societies have you known that have adopted command mechanisms? Why did they do so?
5. What can we say about the relationship between totalitarianism and command economies? Why do you think totalitarian states tend to rely upon command mechanisms?

A Windmill for Animal Farm[10]

In *Animal Farm,* George Orwell described a revolution in which the animals on a farm owned by Mr. Jones rebelled against the oppression of their human masters and drove Mr. Jones and all other human beings away from the place. The leaders of the *coup* were two pigs named Napoleon and Snowball. The revolution was expected to abolish oppression and to establish justice. All animals were to be treated equally: Each would work at what it did best; each would share in the wealth produced by all.

The revolution was betrayed. The animals merely exchanged human masters for animal masters. More and more power came

[10] From *Animal Farm* by George Orwell, copyright, 1946, by Harcourt, Brace & World, Inc., and reprinted with their permission. Pp. 58-59; 65; 67-71; 77-78; 82-86; 107-108; 141-142.

to rest in the hoofs of the two revolutionary leaders. But they could not agree either. They clashed, and Snowball was driven from Animal Farm, leaving Napoleon as the absolute and un-challenged leader of the other animals.

Prior to his purge, Snowball had conceived a plan to build a windmill for the farm, which would ultimately lighten the burden on the animals and bring them a variety of material advantages. Napoleon first opposed the plan, then after Snowball's expulsion adopted it as his own idea. In the first section of the reading which follows, you will learn why Snowball believed the windmill was necessary for Animal Farm. The second and third sections of the reading describe what happened to Snowball's plan after his expulsion.

As you read, consider the following questions:

1. Who decided the goals of Animal Farm's economy?
2. Who decided how resources would be allocated in order to achieve this goal?
3. What did the animals sacrifice to achieve the goal? Why did the animals make these sacrifices?
4. What features reveal that Animal Farm had a command econ-omy?
5. Would the mill have been completed without a command mech-anism? Would it have been completed as soon? Did the command mechanism affect the quality of the windmill?
6. What rewards did the animals receive?

Section I:

"At last the day came when Snowball's plans were completed. At the Meeting on the following Sunday the question of whether or not to begin work on the windmill was to be put to the vote. When the animals had assembled in the big barn, Snowball stood up and, though occasionally interrupted by bleating from the sheep, set forth his reasons for advocating the building of the windmill. Then Napoleon stood up to reply. He said very quietly that the windmill was nonsense and that he advised nobody to vote for it, and promptly sat down again; he had spoken for barely thirty seconds, and seemed almost indifferent as to the effect he produced. At this Snowball sprang to his feet, and shouting down the sheep, who had begun bleating again, broke into a passionate appeal in favour of the windmill. Until now the animals had been about equally divided in their sympathies, but in a moment Snowball's eloquence had carried them away. In glowing sentences he painted a picture of Animal Farm as it might be when sordid labour was lifted from the animals' backs. His imagination had run far beyond chaff-cutters and turnip-slicers. Electricity, he said, could operate threshing machines, ploughs, harrows, rollers, and reapers and binders, besides supplying every stall with its own electric light, hot and cold water, and an electric heater. By the time he had finished speaking, there was no doubt as to which way the vote would go."

[It was at this point that Napoleon, supported by a band of vicious dogs, drove Snowball off the farm.]

Section II:

"On the third Sunday after Snowball's expulsion, the animals were somewhat surprised to hear Napoleon announce that the windmill was to be built after all. He did not give any reason for having changed his mind, but merely warned the animals that this extra task would mean very hard work; it might even be necessary to reduce their rations. The plans, however, had all been prepared, down to the last detail. A special committee of pigs had been at work upon them for the past three weeks. The building of the windmill, with various other improvements, was expected to take two years. . . .

"All that year the animals worked like slaves. But they were happy in their work; they grudged no effort or sacrifice, well aware that everything that they did was for the benefit of themselves and those of their kind who would come after them, and not for a pack of idle, thieving human beings.

"Throughout the spring and summer they worked a sixty-hour week, and in August Napoleon announced that there would be work on Sunday afternoons as well. This work was strictly voluntary, but any animal who absented himself from it would have his rations reduced by half. Even so, it was found necessary to leave certain tasks undone. The harvest was a little less successful than in the previous year, and two fields which should have been sown

with roots in the early summer were not sown because the ploughing had not been completed early enough. It was possible to
foresee that the coming winter would be a hard one.

"The windmill presented unexpected difficulties. There was
a good quarry of limestone on the farm, and plenty of sand and
cement had been found in one of the outhouses, so that all the
materials for building were at hand. But the problem the animals
could not at first solve was how to break up the stone into pieces
of suitable size. There seemed no way of doing this except with
picks and crowbars, which no animal could use, because no animal
could stand on his hind legs. Only after weeks of vain effort did
the right idea occur to somebody—namely, to utilise the force of
gravity. Huge boulders, far too big to be used as they were, were
lying all over the bed of the quarry. The animals lashed ropes
round these, and then all together, cows, horses, sheep, any animal
that could lay hold of the rope—even the pigs sometimes joined in
at critical moments—they dragged them with desperate slowness
up the slope to the top of the quarry, where they were toppled
over the edge, to shatter to pieces below. Transporting the stone
when it was once broken was comparatively simple. The horses
carried it off in cart-loads, the sheep dragged single blocks, even
Muriel and Benjamin yoked themselves into an old governess-cart
and did their share. By late summer a sufficient store of stone had
accumulated, and then the building began, under the super-
intendence of the pigs.

"But it was a slow, laborious process. Frequently it took a whole
day of exhausting effort to drag a single boulder to the top of the
quarry, and sometimes when it was pushed over the edge it failed
to break. Nothing could have been achieved without Boxer,
whose strength seemed equal to that of all the rest of the animals
put together. When the boulder began to slip and the animals
cried out in despair at finding themselves dragged down the
hill, it was always Boxer who strained himself against the rope
and brought the boulder to a stop. To see him toiling up the
slope inch by inch, his breath coming fast, the tips of his hoofs
clawing at the ground, and his great sides matted with sweat,
filled everyone with admiration. Clover warned him sometimes to

be careful not to overstrain himself, but Boxer would never listen to her. His two slogans, 'I will work harder' and 'Napoleon is always right,' seemed to him a sufficient answer to all problems. He had made arrangements with the cockerel to call him three-quarters of an hour earlier in the mornings instead of half an hour. And in his spare moments, of which there were not many nowadays, he would go alone to the quarry, collect a load of broken stone, and drag it down to the site of the windmill unassisted.

"The animals were not badly off throughout that summer, in spite of the hardness of their work. If they had no more food than they had had in Jones's day, at least they did not have less. The advantage of only having to feed themselves, and not having to support five extravagant human beings as well, was so great that it would have taken a lot of failures to outweigh it. And in many ways the animal method of doing things was more efficient and saved labour. Such jobs as weeding, for instance, could be done with a thoroughness impossible to human beings. And again, since no animal now stole, it was unnecessary to fence off pasture from arable land, which saved a lot of labour on the upkeep of hedges and gates. Nevertheless, as the summer wore on, various unforeseen shortages began to make themselves felt. There was need of paraffin oil, nails, string, dog biscuits, and iron for the horses' shoes, none of which could be produced on the farm. Later there would also be need for seeds and artificial manures, besides various tools and, finally, the machinery for the windmill. How these were to be procured, no one was able to imagine.

"One Sunday morning, when the animals assembled to receive their orders, Napoleon announced that he had decided upon a new policy. From now onwards Animal Farm would engage in trade with the neighbouring farms: not, of course, for any commercial purpose, but simply in order to obtain certain materials which were urgently necessary. The needs of the windmill must override everything else, he said. He was therefore making arrangements to sell a stack of hay and part of the current year's wheat crop, and later on, if more money were needed, it would have to be made up by the sale of eggs, for which there was always a market in Willingdon. The hens, said Napoleon, should welcome this sacrifice as their own special contribution towards the building of the windmill. . . .

"By the autumn the animals were tired but happy. They had had a hard year, and after the sale of part of the hay and corn, the stores of food for the winter were none too plentiful, but the windmill compensated for everything. It was almost half built now. After the harvest there was a stretch of clear dry weather, and the animals toiled harder than ever, thinking it well worth while to plod to and fro all day with blocks of stone if by doing so they could raise the walls another foot. Boxer would even come out at nights and work for an hour or two on his own by the light of the harvest moon. In their spare moments the animals would walk round and round the half-finished mill, admiring the strength and perpendicularity of its walls and marvelling that they should ever have been able to build anything so imposing."

[Unfortunately, the animals were to face new frustrations and more sacrifices before the windmill was completed. During a violent November storm, the windmill was blown apart. The walls proved too weak to withstand the force of the storm. Napoleon immediately ordered the building of a new and stronger windmill, and the animals returned to their task of building.]

Section III:

"It was a bitter winter. The stormy weather was followed by sleet and snow, and then by a hard frost which did not break till well into February. The animals carried on as best they could with the rebuilding of the windmill, well knowing that the outside world was watching them and that the envious human beings would rejoice and triumph if the mill were not finished on time. . . .

"In January food fell short. The corn ration was drastically reduced, and it was announced that an extra potato ration would be issued to make up for it. Then it was discovered that the greater part of the potato crop had been frosted in the clamps, which had not been covered thickly enough. The potatoes had become soft and discoloured, and only a few were edible. For days at a time the animals had nothing to eat but chaff and mangels. Starvation seemed to stare them in the face. . . .

". . . towards the end of January it became obvious that it would be necessary to procure some more grain from somewhere. . . .

"One Sunday morning Squealer announced that the hens, who had just come in to lay again, must surrender their eggs. Napoleon had accepted . . . a contract for four hundred eggs a week. The price of these would pay for enough grain and meal to keep the farm going till summer came on and conditions were easier.

"When the hens heard this, they raised a terrible outcry. They had been warned earlier that this sacrifice might be necessary, but had not believed that it would really happen. They were just getting their clutches ready for the spring sitting, and they protested that to take the eggs away now was murder. For the first time since the expulsion of Jones, there was something resembling a rebellion. Led by three young Black Minorca pullets, the hens made a determined effort to thwart Napoleon's wishes. Their method was to fly up to the rafters and there lay their eggs, which smashed to pieces on the floor. Napoleon acted swiftly and ruthlessly. He ordered the hens' rations to be stopped, and decreed that any animal giving so much as a grain of corn to a hen should be punished by death. The dogs saw to it that these orders were carried out. For five days the hens held out, then they capitulated and went back to their nesting boxes. Nine hens had died in the meantime. Their bodies were buried in the orchard, and it was given out that they had died of coccidiosis. . . .

"In the autumn, by a tremendous, exhausting effort—for the harvest had to be gathered at almost the same time—the windmill was finished. The machinery had still to be installed, . . . but the structure was completed. In the teeth of every difficulty, in spite of inexperience, of primitive implements, of bad luck and of Snowball's treachery, the work had been finished punctually to the very day! Tired out but proud, the animals walked round and round their masterpiece, which appeared even more beautiful in their eyes than when it had been built the first time. Moreover, the walls were twice as thick as before. Nothing short of explosives would lay them low this time! And when they thought of how they had laboured, what discouragements they had overcome, and the enormous difference that would be made in their lives when the sails were turning and the dynamos running—when they thought of all this, their tiredness forsook them and they gambolled round and round the windmill, uttering cries of triumph. Napoleon himself, attended by his dogs and his cockerel, came down to inspect the completed work; he personally congratulated the animals on their achievement, and announced that the mill would be named Napoleon Mill."

[Shortly after the completion of the windmill Animal Farm was invaded by jealous neighbors. Although the animals were able to drive the invaders from their land, their windmill was destroyed. Napoleon ordered that a new one be built in its place. In a few years it was completed.]

Section IV:

"The farm was more prosperous now, and better organised: it had even been enlarged by two fields which had been bought from Mr. Pilkington. The windmill had been successfully completed at last, and the farm possessed a threshing machine and a hay elevator of its own, and various new buildings had been added to it. . . . The windmill, however, had not after all been used for generating electrical power. It was used for milling corn, and brought in a handsome money profit. The animals were hard at work building yet another windmill; when that one was finished, so it was said, the dynamos would be installed. But the luxuries of which Snowball had once taught the animals to dream, the stalls with electric light and hot and cold water, and the three-day week, were no longer talked about. Napoleon had denounced such ideas as contrary to the spirit of Animalism. The truest happiness, he said, lay in working hard and living frugally."

Outline of Lesson Plan

First day is used to review basic principles of economics. What are the basic economic questions which all societies must face? What are the basic characteristics of tradition, command, and market systems?

Students read the excerpt from *Animal Farm*. They consider the questions accompanying the reading as they study.

Class discussion around questions for students and those provided for the teacher.

Students draw relationships between a command economic system and totalitarian regimes.

Students formulate Generalization 3.

Estimated time required for this lesson: two days.

Generalization No. 4

Totalitarian states are characterized by single party political systems. Party membership is limited to those who are willing to be unquestionably loyal to the party leaders. Party interest and control encompass all aspects of the society.

Membership in the political party of a one-party, totalitarian state is quite different from party membership in the United States. An American generally assumes no responsibilities or obligations to the party of his choice. He pays no dues nor does he become responsible for party debts. He has no special duties to perform. He need not solicit votes, attend party rallies, or even vote for party candidates if he chooses not to do so. The party had nothing to say about his becoming a member, and if he becomes disgusted and chooses to bolt one party for another, he need not inform either of his choice. Although the majority of adult Americans profess attachment to one political party or another, only about ten per cent actually spend time and money on party affairs.

Membership in a totalitarian party is quite a different thing. In this case only the most dedicated applicants are accepted into full membership after a period of trial. Members are expected to place the party above all other loyalties including friends and family. They pay dues to the party and are expected to serve wherever the party can use them best. They must be unquestionably obedient to party policy, substituting party conscience for their own. In a one-party state, the individual has no choice among parties. He is selected for membership by the party; his choice is to join or become apolitical since there are no other parties. If he decides to join the party, he is immediately one of the political elite. The opportunities available to him as a party member—both to further himself and to serve his country—are much greater than for non-party citizens.

American and totalitarian parties also differ in function. While totalitarian parties perform the same functions as American parties —selection of and mobilization of support for candidates for elective office, recruitment of people for appointive offices, defining of issues, and settlement of conflicts—totalitarian parties are responsible for many other aspects of society as well. A totalitarian party controls all forms of mass communication; it directs the army and police; it supervises all social organizations such as schools, churches, unions, and professional organizations; and it plans and directs the economy. Nothing within the society escapes the attention of a totalitarian party.

SUGGESTED PROCEDURE

The skit which follows may be used to prompt speculation about the nature of a totalitarian party. The teacher may choose six boys to perform the skit before the class. The skit describes a hypothetical meeting of the Executive Committee of the Soviet Communist Party at the local level. Since Russian terms are certain to be unfamiliar to most high school students, American equivalents have been substituted wherever logical and possible.

The skit is not intended to be an accurate portrayal of how an actual party meeting might be run. This little drama is designed only to illustrate some of the functions of the Soviet Communist Party and to describe the degree of commitment and loyalty expected of Party members in the USSR. By focusing on these two aspects—functions of a political party and personal commitment to the party—students can later compare political parties in totalitarian systems with those in the United States.

The teacher may duplicate copies of the script from the guide. The six players should be given their scripts sometime in advance so that they can study and rehearse the skit before they put it on.

You should begin the class period by explaining the setting and purpose of the play. The skit requires approximately 15 minutes to perform. Ask those students who are not acting in the skit to keep a list of functions or activities that seem to occupy the Communist Party. You may find that many students do not understand the notion of "functions," and it might be necessary to allow for fifteen minutes or so of class discussion about the definition of function prior to the playlet. Students should take notes during the playlet. When the skit is completed, use the blackboard or overhead projector to make a list of these functions as they are contributed by the class. When the students seem to have exhausted the list of functions they are able to assign to the party, ask them to list phrases and adjectives which describe the position of party members vis-à-vis the Party. The skit and the listing of functions of the Party and phrases about Party members will take up most or all of the class period.

Students should be able to suggest lists of party functions and party member characteristics which resemble the following:

Activities or functions of the Communist Party	Characteristics of Party members
1. recruit and train party members	1. devoted
2. control various phases of economy—unions, industry, agriculture, etc.	2. loyal
3. control propaganda and communication media	3. absolute obedience
4. control police	4. disciplined
5. control youth activities	5. willingness to sacrifice for party
6. hold elections	6. submerge individual will to party will
7. select candidates for political office	
8. fill appointive posts in government	
9. direct legislation	
10. direct the essential administration of government	

In preparation for class on the following day, ask students to prepare at home two lists on American political parties similar to the two they prepared on the Soviet Communist Party. In one list they should list functions of American parties; in the other, descriptive phrases of American party members. When class begins, the teacher may add the new lists to the blackboard or overhead projector.

The teacher should then encourage students to speculate about the functions of totalitarian political parties as compared to parties in the United States. For example, the teacher may ask: To what degree do political parties assume functions in totalitarian states normally conducted by non-political organizations in the United States? What differences in party functions stem from the fact that our system is based on competition between two major parties while totalitarian states have only one party?

The teacher should also encourage students to reflect on the different demands placed on party members in totalitarian states and in the United States. Why do American parties welcome all citizens as members, and demand little of them while totalitarian parties are very restrictive in membership and demand much of their members?

Near the close of the period encourage students to generalize about the nature of political parties in totalitarian states. They should reach a conclusion very similar to the generalization posed at the beginning of this lesson.

THE PROFESSIONALS

Cast of Characters:

[All are members of the Executive Committee of the Ilyich County branch of the Communist Party of the USSR.]

Chairman Andreyev: middle-aged man; blunt but persuasive; believes duty, obedience, and hard work are most essential ingredients for a party member.

First Secretary Belinsky: efficient Party member; responsible for recruitment and training of party members; also takes charge of selecting candidates to stand for election; impatient with debate.

Second Secretary Chernov: loyal and obedient Party man; does what he is told; quick to swim with the current.

Head of Secret Police Davidov: sits on edge of group; speaks little but appears to know much more than he is willing to discuss; when he does speak, he does so without humor or strong passion.

Head of Young Communist League Egorov: Youngest of group; tends to be flippant; tries to be humorous; does not appear to take matters as seriously as others; visibly uncomfortable when the scandal in the Young Communist League is mentioned.

Head of Propaganda and Communication Golikov: a busy person; speaks quickly and often; filled with importance of his job and the tasks of the Party generally.

Stage Setting:

The six members are seated at a large table—four along one side, and one on each end—facing the class. Andreyev and Belinsky sit near the middle of the table; Egorov and Golikov are seated at the ends of the table. On the wall behind them are pictures of Lenin, Leonid Brezhnev and Alexei Kosygin. Andreyev holds a gavel; Chernov has papers from which he reads the minutes of the last meeting.

Chairman Andreyev: (gaveling) The meeting of the Executive Committee of the Soviet Communist Party of Ilyich County will come to order. Comrade Chernov will read the minutes of our last meeting.

Chernov: The Executive Committee met on March 1 to conduct routine business. First Secretary Belinsky reported on progress in the recruitment of Party leaders. Comrade Belinsky noted a number of problems relating to recruitment. It is becoming increasingly difficult to secure new members who are not merely joining for the purpose of advancing their own careers. The importance of Party membership to secure important posts in the political and economic life of our country is obvious to most of our citizens. Therefore, many are prompted to join who have little of the revolutionary fervor that once marked our Party members, but who wish only to add to their own material comfort. They are putting individual interests before the goals of socialism. Furthermore, we are falling behind in the relative proportion of peasants and workers who enter our Party. The Communist Party was built upon the working classes; now it is being filled with intellectuals.

A second problem that was discussed . . .

Andreyev: Before you go on, I think the minutes should contain some mention of the discussion relating to the class nature of new Party members. It was agreed by everyone that intellectuals were not being opposed as a matter of principle. Many of our best educated Party leaders had their origins in the factories or on the farms. The issue is simply this: our Party must always be concerned that all ethnic and occupational groups are duly represented. Members should be drawn from the military, the arts, the sciences, managerial classes, and the workers—be they peasant or industrial. How else can our Party be said to represent all Russians? We are all aware that social classes as known in the West no longer exist in Russia; however, there are differences among occupational and educational groups and all should be properly represented in the Party. Nevertheless we are not interested in adding large numbers of new members to our Party. Lenin himself said that only the most dedicated revolutionaries should be permitted to join. The fact that only 7-10 percent of the adult population is allowed to join the Party is as it should be. It is both a privilege and a great responsibility to become a Communist. Go on—

Chernov: Thank you. I shall note these additions to the minutes.

A second problem that was discussed was a dispute which had arisen at the Lenin overshoe factory. As you know. the machine that stamps out the overshoe for the left foot broke down. The machine requires considerable repair and parts are presently unavailable. Comrade Kabanov, the head of the agricultural sector, asked that the workers assigned to produce left overshoes be assigned to farmwork as help was in short supply. Levitsky, the manager of the Lenin plant, opposed this idea. He insisted that he had his quota to fulfill. By working double shifts, he could produce twice as many overshoes for the right foot than had been originally planned. By dividing this in two to account for the absence of left shoes, he would just about equal his assigned target of pairs of overshoes. But to do this, he needed all his men.

The decision of the Executive Committee was to transfer one-half of the idle industrial workers to farm work on a temporary basis, the other half remaining at the factory to repair the broken machine and to be available for work as substitutes when needed. Levitsky was reprimanded for being more interested in his year-end bonus for fulfilling the plan than for rational production of needed consumer goods. Meanwhile the Executive Committee has sent a letter to the Central Planning Bureau in Moscow alerting them to the breakdown and urging that parts be sent as rapidly as possible.

The final item of business concerned a report by Comrade Davidov, head of the Ilyich County Secret Police. [*All glance at Egorov who is visibly uncomfortable.*] His investigators have learned that certain members of the Young Communist League are engaged in illegal purchases and sales of Western clothing, books, jazz records, and art objects. These are obtained from

American tourists and sold to college students and young hooligans. Comrade Egorov, head of the Young Communist League, appeared unaware of this scandal in his own department but promised to look into the matter. The Executive Committee decided the evidence was conclusive; it was beyond the stage of "looking into." Debate centered on whether the culprits should be brought to public trial as common criminals or treated differently because of their membership in the Young Communist League. The decision was that the accused should be expelled from the Young Communist League and tried as criminals as a lesson to other members who might feel the urge to take advantage of their privileged status. That concludes the reading of the minutes, Comrade.

Andreyev: Very good! Are there any questions? No? Very well. We shall hear a report from First Secretary Belinsky regarding the coming elections to the Supreme Soviet—our national legislative body.

Belinksy: As is customary I asked the various labor unions, collective farms, military organizations and others to suggest nominees for one who would stand for election as the deputy to represent Ilyich County in the Supreme Soviet. Each group met; most offered nominations. The majority of organizations nominated Chairman Andreyev of our Executive Committee. Other names familiar to you were put forward, but one in particular caught my eye. This was the name of Anna Mikhailovna Petrovsky of the Red Star Collective Farm. She was nominated by her peasant colleagues for her unusual heroism in rescuing livestock during the flood last year. Each of you know her by name if not by face.

Golikov: We all know Anna Mikhailovna and are proud of her devotion to duty. But she is not a Communist. She is only a peasant girl. Should we not put forward one of our own colleagues who has given loyal service to the Party?

Belinsky: In recent years our candidates have generally been Party members. But this was not always true. There have been factory workers, school teachers and Comrade Sokolnikov was a doctor when he was elected.

Davidov: I have checked her record and her associations. I can assure you she has done nothing in the past which would embarrass us or the Party.

Egorov: (*Flippantly*) I say nominate her. We all know it is an empty honor anyway. What does it matter whom we send. All decisions are made by our Party leaders and not by the deputies in the Supreme Soviet. The deputies merely endorse what has already been decided in the Party Councils.

Andreyev: *(Sternly)* Not so fast, comrade. Election to the Supreme Soviet is indeed an honor and is not to be treated lightly. It is true that our Party exercises a directing role and that no important political or organizational question is decided by the Soviets without directions from the Party. Nevertheless, we should send only those deputies who are deserving of the honor to represent our county in the national legislature. Naturally major policy decisions must be made by those familiar with the day-to-day operations of the country, but this makes it no less important to send loyal and honorable deputies to represent our citizens.

Belinsky: I have checked the name of Anna Mikhailovna with Moscow. They have examined her record and believe she would be a good choice. Finally, they like the idea of our sending a woman and a peasant for a change.

Andreyev: Since Moscow has approved and there are no objections, Anna Mikhailovna will be listed as our nominee for election to the Supreme Soviet. Now, what about preparations for the election? This is your department, Comrade Golikov.

Golikov: Plans are already under way. All newspapers, magazines, radio and T.V. stations have been alerted to the theme of this election campaign which is "Catch and Overtake the West in the Production of Consumer Goods." Large posters have been ordered from Moscow which compare our rate of economic growth to that of the United States. Recorded speeches by our Party leaders will be played daily on radio and television. These talks will describe our accomplishments and explain the kinds of sacrifices that are still required. Articles for newspapers were prepared long ago in Moscow for this election and have been circulated to all newspapers throughout the country. They are ready to go to print when the election campaign begins. On the day before the election there will be a large parade in which children will carry flags. Older youth will carry pictures of our party leaders.

Egorov: *(In a jesting manner)* Don't you think it might be necessary to say something about Anna Mikhailovna and show her picture somewhere? She might not be elected, you know. *(laugh)*

Andreyev: *(Soberly)* We can do without your flip comments, Comrade. She will be the only nominee. How can she fail to be elected? Go on, Comrade Golikov.

Golikov: Of course, there will be some pictures of Anna Mikhailovna and a description of her heroic labor, but this part of our campaign will require little effort.

Chernov: What about the election itself? What have you done to guarantee a large turnout?

Golikov: Obviously, the campaign is expected to build interest and enthusiasm. On election day itself, all workers will be given a half-day with pay. Trucks will bring workers from factories, mines, and farms to the polling booths. For those who are in hospitals or bed-fast at home, election workers will take a ballot to their homes. Checkers have been assigned to each block in the cities to make certain all eligible residents vote. We should do even better than the last turnout of 99 percent.

Andreyev: Very good comrade. Are there questions any of you wish to ask him? We shall expect additional progress reports as the day of the election approaches. There is one final item of business. Comrade Egorov has been relieved of his duties as head of the Young Communist League and it . . .

Egorov: (*Jumping to his feet*) What! When! On what grounds!

Andreyev: (*Quietly but firmly*) Sit down and be quiet comrade! [*Egorov sits down.*] . . . and it will be necessary to begin a search for his replacement.

Egorov: (*Speaking sharply and with emotion*) I demand to know why I'm being *replaced* and where I am to be *transferred!* I knew nothing of this!

Andreyev: Your complete record in the Communist Party including the most recent scandal which occurred in the Young Communist League right under your very nose has been brought to the attention of the highest officials of the Party. We are agreed that you have been derelict in your duty. The fact that you did not report the illegal activity taking place within your own organization first caused us to believe that you too must be sharing in the crime. Later, we learned that you were guilty only of stupidity, incompetence, and arrogance. You were given a job to do for the Party, comrade, and you failed. You have disgraced us, and you must be punished.

Egorov: (*Subdued but protesting*) I admit that I should have detected the gangs involved in the black market before they were discovered by the Secret Police. But my failure could have happened to anyone. Those hooligans were clever. I . . .

Andreyev: No, Comrade, such errors do not happen to everyone. They happen to those who are not sufficiently devoted to the Party to give their full attention to their assigned responsibilities. These mistakes are made by people who look upon Party work as a sideline or a hobby, not as a way of life. I have watched you for some time, Comrade. You are proud, even arrogant. You make flippant comments in our Party sessions just as you have today. You are filled with suggestions; you always think you know a better way to do something than our Party leaders. You failed in your responsibility because you are too filled with yourself. You always put Egorov ahead of the Party.

Egorov: Not so, Comrade. I admit my blindness to the crime in the Young Communist League, but it was not as you say. I've always been loyal to the Party. If I sometimes criticize Party directives, it is because I think we should be as efficient as possible. Surely, the overshoe case proves we have much to learn about efficiency.

Andreyev: (*Becoming more angry*) You talk of efficiency while you let the blackmarket grow like bindweed in your own cornfield. Efficiency is important, but first comes loyalty, responsibility, and obedience to the Party.

Davidov: (*Heatedly*) What does Egorov know of Party loyalty and obedience? We who went through the revolution gave freely of our lives and property to save the Party. No sacrifice was too great. We pledged our lives and fortunes to build a new and glorious socialist Russia.

Belinsky: What is guilt after all? The young hooligans traded illegally on the black market because they had a fool for a leader. They would not have dared traffic in tourist clothes if there had been a true Party man in charge of them.

Golikov: (*With indignation*) Why do such scandals occur? They occur wherever there is a Party member more interested in advancing himself than the Party. It is people like you that we must weed out of the Party. You simply use Party membership to gain privileges for you and your family—privileges without any of the sacrifice.

Chernov: (*Vindictively*) We should not even permit people like you to remain in the Party. What do you contribute?

Egorov: (*Without anger and in a rational tone of voice*) I contribute my loyalty and obedience. But I contribute something more— my ideas. Lenin himself coined the term "democratic centralism." He recognized the need for democratic discussion.

Chernov: (*Testily*) Democracy! You don't know the first thing about Communist democracy! Your democracy consists of flip comments and smug asides such as the kind of contributions you made in the meeting today. We can do without your carping, criticism, and clever words. The Party needs unity of will. The job to be done is an immense one. We can succeed only if all members voluntarily thrust their shoulders to the wheel and push. You and others like you stand in our way. You must stand aside or begin to work with the rest of us. If you persist as you have, we will run over you.

Egorov: (*With more feeling*) In what sense have I been in the way? True, I've made mistakes; but none of us is perfect. You'll recall my suggestions regarding the collection of membership dues resulted in savings for our Party. The Party neither needs nor wants automatons. It needs men able to think and to act. We are not puppets to be pulled about on strings.

Davidov: Quite true, comrade. No one asks you to be a puppet. Nor do you have to remain a Party member. But once you made the decision to join the Party you pledged yourself to make the Party will your will, the Party views your views. How could we have accomplished all that we have in Russia since the revolution if we permitted ourselves to be diverted from our course by individual views or endless discussions? How could the collectivization of agriculture ever have been accomplished if we had stopped to debate each decision or to pacify each individual who raised a question?

Egorov: But what of imagination and initiative?

Belinsky: (*Rationally*) There is adequate opportunity for imagination and initiative comrade. You can look for better and more efficient ways for carrying out policies decreed from above.

Chernov: (*Angrily*) What conceit you have to think that your opinion, your views, your limited experience are superior to that of the collective opinion, view, and experience of the entire Party. Our leaders have been tested by revolution, war, and endless struggle. Think for a moment, comrade—what would have happened in the revolution or during the Civil War if we had been led by bunglers and incompetents like you. At one time, your mistake and carelessness would have earned you a prison sentence if not a firing squad. You are guilty, comrade, guilty of allowing criminals to operate in your own department. Your failure was brought about by foolish pride and conceit.

Egorov: (*Visibly shaken; apologetic but not groveling*) Stop, please stop, comrades! . . . I've failed you, failed the Party, failed my country. You are right. If I had spent more time looking to my responsibilities and less time day-dreaming about how to improve the Party, the scandal would never have occurred. I joined the Party because I believe in its mission. At times I foolishly criticized Party policy because I thought I knew better than our leaders. I was stupid and conceited. I know the Party is always right. I deserve your criticism and anger. You have been patient with me longer than I deserve. I am willing to do anything to correct my mistakes only . . . please don't expel me from the Party. Where would I go? What would I do? Who would want me? How could I face my family and friends? Give me the chance to correct my mistakes and to prove my loyalty to the Party.

Andreyev: (*Kindly but firm*) I believe, Comrade, that you are sincere and deserve another chance. But it will not be easy for you. The Party has decided to transfer you to the eastern lands agricultural project. There you will be in charge of organizing the cultivation of virgin soil. It is a desolate area, demanding the best you have to offer. You will have plenty of opportunity for initiative and imagination there. If you succeed, perhaps in five years the Party will consider your application for a transfer. Do you have any questions?

Egorov: (*Quietly*) None. (*Then more firmly and soberly*) Thank you comrades. I will do my best, and you will come to be proud of me.

Andreyev: The meeting is adjourned!

Outline of Lesson Plan

Six players assigned parts and given scripts.

Class Period I

Introduction to playlet
1. Discussion of the term *function*
2. Instructions about taking notes during the playet

Playlet

Class offers list of functions noted in playlet. Contributions noted on blackboard or overhead projector.

Students list phrases and adjectives which describe the position of party members *vis-à-vis* the Party, e.g., "loyal," "dedicated," etc.

Assigned Homework

Students prepare at home two lists (one of functions, the other of descriptive phrases) on American political parties.

Class Period II

New lists added to blackboard or projector.

Speculation and class discussion about differences between political parties in totalitarian and democratic states.

Students formulate generalization about the nature of political parties in totalitarian states.

Students articulate generalization No. 4 (p. 37).

Estimated time required for this lesson: two days

Generalization No. 5

Totalitarian systems tend to fall to the control of single leaders. These leaders are then made out to be almost superhuman.

In his famous denunciation of Stalin (1956), Khrushchev vividly recounted the powers which a single leader could assume in a system regulated by one party. In a totalitarian state, leadership tends to concentrate in the person of one man; soon the leader has absolute power; he is depicted as a being of extraordinary endowments, whose gifts raise him far above the ordinary man; and his image, the image of a superman, is constantly before the public. Students of totalitarian systems frequently point to the ubiquitous posters of the leader; the photographs displayed in all public buildings and most homes; the statues, monuments, and buildings marked with the name of the leader; and the salutes, ceremonies, and other signs of respect to illustrate the way in which the leader of a totalitarian regime assumes the role of a father, a god, a spokesman for the mass mind.

George Orwell's book *1984* depicts the epitome of totalitarianism and Big Brother the archetype of the totalitarian leader. Just as the society which Orwell fabricated in *1984* illustrates the model, not the actuality, of a totalitarian system, so have the leaders of Nazi Germany, Communist China, or Stalinist Russia, only approximated the image of Big Brother. Nevertheless, the following passage from *1984* describes a role to which totalitarian rulers might aspire.

". . . one could infer, if one did not know it already, the general structure of Oceanic society. At the apex of the pyramid comes

Big Brother. Big Brother is infallible and all-powerful. Every success, every achievement, every victory, every scientific discovery,
all knowledge, all wisdom, all happiness, all virtue, are held to
issue directly from his leadership and inspiration. Nobody has
ever seen Big Brother. He is a face on the hoardings, a voice on
the telescreen. We may be reasonably sure that he will never die,
and there is already considerable uncertainty as to when he was
born. Big Brother is the guise in which the Party chooses to
exhibit itself to the world. His function is to act as a focusing
point for love, fear, and reverence, emotions which are more
easily felt toward an individual than toward an organization.
Below Big Brother comes the Inner Party, its numbers limited to
six millions, or something less than two per cent of the population
of Oceania. Below the Inner Party comes the Outer Party, which,
if the Inner Party is described as the brain of the State, may be
justly likened to the hands. Below that come the dumb masses
whom we habitually refer to as 'the proles,' numbering perhaps
eighty-five per cent of the population."[11]

Suggested Procedure

There are a number of ways in which a teacher can demonstrate
the cult of a leader in a totalitarian state. For example, the
growth of myths that present the leader as one who is more than
human and is to be trusted and followed at all costs, can be illustrated by references to Soviet textbooks. Textbooks have often
been rewritten to stress theretofore unknown deeds of the current
leader and to purge the former leader from the historical record.
Or students might bring to class pictures which show how the
leaders of totalitarian states have been regarded. Back issues of
Life and *Look* magazines contain photographs of mass demonstrations and political rallies in such states as Nazi Germany, Communist China, and Stalinist Russia.

This generalization about totalitarian leadership may be taught
through the use of quotations. What the followers have said about
their leader provides insights into the type of image the leader

[11] From *1984* by George Orwell, copyright, 1949, by Harcourt, Brace & World,
Inc. Reprinted by permission of Brandt & Brandt, p. 209.

sought to project. We can learn if the leader demanded a degree and kind of loyalty and faith which transcended that normally shown toward political leaders.

A series of statements about Adolph Hitler and Josef Stalin appears at the end of this lesson. They can be shown on the overhead projector or be mimeographed and distributed to students.

Students should first read the statements and then decide what characteristics and achievements are attributed to the two leaders. Do you think Germans and Russians believed these statements about their respective leaders? Compare the two lists of statements. Hitler was a Nazi; Stalin a Communist. Presumably they were bitter foes, but do the statements about Hitler appear similar to those concerning Stalin? May we assume that totalitarian leaders, despite their differing ideologies, may aspire to similar positions or roles? You may want to read to your students the passage from *1984* and ask them to compare the description of Big Brother with the quotations about Stalin and Hitler.

If time allows, students can compare the position of a totalitarian leader with that of a leader in a democratic system. Would statements such as those about Stalin and Hitler appear about the President of the United States? What is the traditional role of the "out-party" in the United States? Would the criticism of the "outs" be tolerated in a totalitarian system? How is the President of the United States regarded by members of his own party before he is chosen at the national convention? When he is candidate for office? After he is elected president? What kinds of images have American presidents had for the general public? (Here students might consider figures such as Washington or Lincoln, or more recent figures such as Eisenhower or Kennedy.) How do their images differ from those of totalitarian leaders?

You may also wish to show one or more cartoons which reveal the President or another political leader in a humorous or slightly unfavorable way. Ask students what the cartoons represent about the opportunity to criticize leaders in the United States. Note that leaders of totalitarian states do not permit themselves to be caricatured. When drawings do appear in totalitarian states, they are designed to show the leaders' positive qualities, such as bravery and leadership ability.

At the close of the period the students should be encouraged to put into words what they have learned from this lesson, approximating the meaning of Generalization No. 5.

WHAT THEY SAID ABOUT ADOLPH HITLER AND JOSEF STALIN[12]

Hitler

1. "Formerly, we were in the habit of saying: this is *right or wrong*; today, we must put the question accordingly: *What would the 'Führer' say?* This attitude towards the 'Führer' as well as his own person, are the Categorical Imperative to which German life must henceforth conform. We are under the great obligation of recognizing as a holy work of our Volk's spirit the laws signed by Adolph Hitler's name. Hitler has received his authority from God. Therefore, he is a champion, sent by God, for German Right in the world."

   Reich-Minister of Justice, Hans Frank.

2. "All Germans cry out in this hour: Heil now and in all eternity our fervently loved Führer who alone has made our lives again worth living!"—Hermann Göring.
   (*Reichstag,* 19/3/38.)

3. "Again and again we must be grateful to our fate for having given us that man who, as the incarnation of spirit and action in the German spiritual life, gives new impulses to the German art

Stalin

1. Stalin! Always we hear in our souls his dear name. And here, in the Kremlin, his presence touches us at every step. We walk on stones which he may have trod only recently. Let us fall on our knees and kiss those holy footprints.
   —*From Zemlia Russkaia [Russian Land], book published by Komsomol,* 1946.

2. The heart of every Soviet citizen is warmed by his love of Stalin. In all languages of the world, humanity glorifies his name, the name of the promoter of popular happiness, of the head of working humanity.
   —*Pravda,* December 10, 1949.

3. O Great Stalin, O Leader of the Peoples,
   Thou who didst give birth to man,
   Thou who didst make fertile the earth,

---

[12] The quotations about Stalin were printed in *Problems of Communism,* Vol. XII, No. 2 (March-April, 1963) 87; the first quotation about Hitler appeared in David Spitz, *Patterns of Anti-Democratic Thought.* New York: The Macmillan Company, 1949, p. 223; the balance of the Hitler quotes are from the *Nazi Guide to Nazism,* ed. by Rolf Tell. Washington, D.C.: American Council on Public Affairs, 1942, pp. 186-187.

Hitler

and creates real internal liberty."
(*Der Angriff*, 7/9/34.)

4. "For all this we owe a great debt of gratitude to our Führer, Adolf Hitler, the creator of a German art and civilization."—Adolf Wagner, State Minister.
(*Reception of Foreign Press, Nymphenburg*, 9/7/38.)

5. "Life in National Socialist Germany has become more beautiful. Adolf Hitler's Germany is great and powerful as never before. Our immortal people becomes nobler and better from day to day."—Proclamation, Dr. Robert Ley.
(*Proclamation to National Festival*, 1/5/38.)

6. "The great orators and writers of a nation are, in fact, the creators of its language. Our Führer stands as an ideal model of this creative power before our eyes. His language is, in the best sense of the word, real language creation."—Dr. Goebbels.
(*Annual Meeting Reich Cultural Chamber*, 25/11/38.)

7. "How may I find words for your deeds? Has any mortal being ever loved so much as you, my Führer? Has any faith ever been as strong as that in your mission? God sent you to us for Germany"—Hermann Göring.
(*Reichstag*, 19/3/38.)

8. "We live again! We, having been ill, have recovered our health! The Führer has guided us like a convalescent. It is a miracle, and our Lord blesses this man, our

Stalin

Thou who dost rejuvenate the centuries,
Thou who givest blossom to the spring . . .
—*Pravda*, August 28, 1936.

4. He personally . . .
. . . [was responsible] for planting eucalyptus treees on the coast of the Black Sea, cultivating melons in the Moscow region and extending the cultivation of branched wheat.
—*Pravda*, December 21, 1949.

5. He personally . . .
. . . inspires Soviet male and female physical culturists to achieve new successes in sport for the glory of the great socialist Homeland.
—*Pravda*, May 26, 1952.

6. He is . . .
. . . the creator of the Soviet Armed Forces, the great military leader of modern times . . . the creator of the progressive Soviet military science. . . .
—*N. Bulganin in Pravda*, December 21, 1949.

7. He is . . .
. . . the greatest Marxist, the great Leninist, the brilliant continuer of the great cause of Marx-Engels-Lenin. . . .
—*Soviet State and Law*, No. 4, 1950, p. 79.

8. He is friend of the sun
He will disarm all his foes.
Your name is on our lips,
Your heart is in our hearts,
Your will in our deeds.

Hitler	Stalin
Führer, Adolf Hitler."—Dr. Robert Ley.	Stalin, the father, has sixteen daughters—
(Proclamation to National Festival, 1/15/37.)	Sixteen loving Republics.
	—*Pravda*, December 11, 1949.

OUTLINE OF LESSON PLAN

Quotations about Hitler and Stalin are displayed on blackboard, overhead projector, or mimeographed sheets.

Class evaluates reputed attributes and achievements of Hitler and Stalin.

Class compares "Hitler statements" with "Stalin statements."

Students formulate generalizations about leader in a totalitarian system, and compare their views with the description of Big Brother.

Optional: Comparison of position of leaders in democratic and totalitarian systems.

Students bring pictures, cartoons, or other statements to class for discussion.

Estimated time required for lesson: one day.

Generalization No. 6

Totalitarian regimes are characterized by a commitment to a specific ideology. The ideology serves the state by defining the past, explaining the present, and predicting the future. It establishes guidelines for remolding society in the image held by the rulers. To the degree that the ideology is accepted by the mass of population, it can inspire dedication and loyalty to the regime.

Every individual finds it necessary to fit his experiences and observations into a more or less coherent body of belief. We commonly refer to this as one's "personal philosophy of life." To a large degree it *is* "personal," because the essence of one's world view is conditioned by highly personal experiences. Whether a person is trustful or suspicious in his business relationships depends largely upon the nature of his experience and what he has been told to expect. Our personal philosophy, therefore, determines in large part how we view previous events, current happenings, and future possibilities.

Nevertheless, no individual's philosophy is wholly his own. One acquires attitudes and beliefs similar to those of others in his environment. A citizen of a small town might react unfavorably to large cities; a midwesterner might be hostile to the east; or an American suspicious of foreigners.

Each of us has a kind of personal ideology which might be defined as a reasonably coherent body of ideas which determines how we act. In a free and open society myriads of such ideologies compete for attention. No single group is able to impose its beliefs on others. While adhering to our own ideas, we have continuous communication with those who follow different beliefs. This cross-fertilization of beliefs can serve to make us more tolerant and perhaps more willing to adjust our philosophy to changing circumstances or personal needs. The slogan "make the world safe for democracy" was attractive precisely because it meant so many different things to different people. Many Americans felt that it affirmed precisely the right to be different and to believe what one chose.

Ideology is not unique to totalitarian states; all states and all individuals have ideologies loosely defined. What is different about totalitarianism, however, is that totalitarian states have a prescribed ideology to which all citizens must conform. The marketplace of ideas is closed to make way for a rigid code of belief fostered by the state. All groups that might compete with the state—e.g., churches, civic associations, schools, youth groups—come under intense attack and pressure to conform. The individual is not deprived of belief. Quite the contrary! Belief and faith are encouraged; but his belief must be like his neighbor's, which is the same as their political leader's beliefs. There is one code, one approved philosophy.

Ideology serves a number of functions for a totalitarian regime. The official texts printed and circulated by the state delineate codes of ethics and morality, an interpretation of the past, the requirements of the present, and the goals to which all citizens must aspire. The official ideology defines the enemies of the regime and discloses what is necessary for one to be accepted as an ally. Not only is the individual expected to accept the ideology, he is also expected to be enthusiastic and loudly support its ideas. In brief, totalitarian ideologies may be viewed as secularized religions, demanding the kind of commitment that was expected of Christians during the Middle Ages.

It is important for a study of totalitarianism that students learn the purposes ideologies serve in a totalitarian state. A teacher may want his students to know something about totalitarian ideologies—e.g., Marxism-Leninism—but that is not the purpose of this lesson. This lesson seeks to demonstrate that:

1. Totalitarian regimes have well-defined ideologies.
2. These ideologies generate enthusiasm and vigorous support among their converts.
3. Totalitarian ideologies serve a variety of functions, including defining the past, explaining the present, and predicting the future.
4. Totalitarian ideologies bear marked resemblances to theologies. They are absolute in their analyses; they promise rewards for faithful service; they establish the rules for moral and ethical conduct.
5. Totalitarian ideologies validate the actions of their regime. To oppose a totalitarian regime which is furthering the ideology is to side with evil against good.

SUGGESTED PROCEDURE

This lesson is based upon an authentic letter written by a young American Communist. To disguise his identity from the students, numbered blanks have been inserted in place of key words.

You may duplicate the letter and distribute copies to the class. The students are to read the entire letter and then see if they can guess the author's identity—not by name of course—but by association. For example, is he a school teacher, a Buddhist, etc.? Insist that students read the entire letter and try to capture the spirit and attitude of the writer before they make their decisions. When students think that they have identified him, they should fill in the blanks with terms appropriate to their identification decision.

Reading the letter and filling in the blanks will require about 15 minutes. When the class has finished, ask individual students to tell you what choices they made regarding the writer's identity. You will get many answers, including the following: Communist, Socialist, Christian, Peace Corps worker, civil rights worker, missionary, Nazi, Black Muslim. As students contribute their answers, write them on the board. Then tell the class that you will give them a hint: the young man is an American; also, point to the footnote on the bottom of the first page of the letter. With this information some students will want to change their answers from Communist to Christian.

At this point tell the class that the letter was written by a Communist, and give them the correct answers to all the blanks. Point to the list of answers contributed by the class and ask why there were so many other possibilities. For example, why was this young American Communist taken for a Christian, a civil rights worker, and so on? Since the students may be unable to articulate the reasons for their choices of labels, you might ask them to glance over the letter again and suggest a number of adjectives which seem to describe the author of the letter. Students will offer such responses as devoted, fanatical, committed, believing, irrational, dedicated, and radical. Ask if any or all of the adjectives they suggest fit the categories of individuals they suggested earlier. They will quickly see that dedication, loyalty, or devotion can be characteristics of a Christian, for example, as well as of a Communist.

You might have your students compare the functions of theology and ideology. A theology defines the past and describes the future; it establishes the norms for moral conduct; it clarifies the believer's goals; it provides the convert with a sense of purpose; and theology offers the believer rewards or punishments for behavior which follows or conflicts with religious tenets. Students can quickly identify passages from the letter that indicate that Communist ideology performs similar functions for the letter writer.

Finally, ask the class: What advantages would totalitarian regimes gain if all their citizens were as committed to a specific ideology as this young Communist is to his? From this question and from those discussed before, students should be able to reach a conclusion approximating that stated in the generalization for this lesson.

Answers to the blanks in the reading
1. Communist, 2. socialist, 3. socialism, 4. socialist, 5. radical, 6. party, 7. class, 8. Radicals, 9. socialism, 10. communists, 11. capitalist, 12. religious, 13. party.

LETTER FROM A YOUNG (1)_____ [13]

"What seems of first importance to you is to me either not desirable or impossible of realization. But there is one thing about which I am in dead earnest—and that is the (2)_____ cause. It is my life, my business, my religion, my hobby, my sweetheart, wife, and mistress, my bread and meat. I work at it in the daytime and dream of it at night. Its hold on me grows, not lessens, as time goes on. I'll be in it the rest of my life. It is my alter-ego. When you think of me, it is necessary to think of (3)_____ as well, because I'm inseparably bound to it.

"Therefore I can't carry on a friendship, a love affair, or even a conversation without relating it to this force which both drives and guides my life. I evaluate people, books, ideas, and notions according to how they affect the (4) _____ cause and by their attitude toward it.

"I have already been in jail because of my ideas, and if necessary I am ready to go before a firing squad. A certain percentage of us get killed or imprisoned. Even for those who escape these harsher ends, life is no bed of roses. A genuine (5)_____ lives in virtual poverty. He turns back to the (6) _____ every penny he makes above what is absolutely necessary to keep him alive. We constantly look for places where the (7) _____ struggle is the sharpest, exploiting these situations to the limit of their possibilities. We lead strikes. We organize demonstrations. We speak on street corners. We fight cops. We go through trying experiences many times each year which the ordinary man has to face only once or twice in a lifetime.

"And when we're not doing these more exciting things, all our spare time is taken up with dull routine chores, endless leg work, errands, etc., which are inescapably connected with running a live organization.

"(8)_____ don't have the time or the money for many movies or concerts or T-bone steaks or decent homes and new cars. We've been described as fanatics. We are. Our lives are dominated by one great, overshadowing factor—the struggle for (9)_____.

---

[13] *Presbyterian Survey* (February, 1961) p. 1.

"Well, that's what my life is going to be. That's the black side of it. Then there is the other side of it. We (10)_____ have a philosophy of life which no amount of money could buy. We have a cause to fight for, a definite purpose in life. We subordinate our petty personal selves into a great movement of humanity. We have a morale, an *esprit de corps* such as no (11)_____ army ever had; we have a code of conduct, a way of life, a devotion to our cause that no (12)_____ order can touch. And we are guided not by blind, fanatical faith but by logic and reason, by a never-ending education of study and practice.

"And if our personal lives seem hard or our egos appear to suffer through subordination to the (13)_____, then we are adequately compensated by the thought that each of us is in his small way helping to contribute something new and true, something better to mankind."

OUTLINE OF LESSON PLAN

Mimeographed copies of letter distributed to class.

Students fill in blanks. Teacher lists identification labels on the board. Class told that author is an American.

Discussion about new labels.

Author identified and correct answers to blanks listed.

Teacher lists on the board the adjectives which students believe describe the author.

Class discusses the applicability of adjectives to previously-listed labels.

Discussion centers on a functional comparison of theology and ideology. Students led to see that ideology serves a number of functions for an individual and for a totalitarian state.

Students led to formulate generalization similar to that beginning the lesson.

Estimated time required for this lesson: one day

Generalization No. 7

A totalitarian state seeks to subordinate all social institutions to the control of the state and thereby removes all possible challengers to its control. No human activity is without interest to totalitarian rulers. To control the behavior of its citizens, totalitarian regimes recognize no limits to the means which may be employed to achieve their ends.

Thus far we have examined the concern totalitarian rulers have for politics and economics. But totalitarianism does not end with politics and economics; a totalitarian system seeks to control the "total" life of its subjects. The family, church, schools, professional associations, civic organizations, the military, and others are all subject to the web of the regime. In some totalitarian states, certain of these institutions appear to have retained a degree of autonomy. But these institutions—such as the family, churches, universities, and the military which Carl Friedrich and Zbigniew Brzezinski refer to as "islands of separateness"—are continually threatened.

Totalitarian rulers are not only interested in controlling the organized and individual behavior of their citizens, they seek also to control the very thoughts of their subjects. Although totalitarian regimes thus far have apparently failed to capture the minds of all citizens, they have not been discouraged from making the effort. Ranging from "friendly persuasion" to the use of terror, the totalitarian arsenal of manipulative techniques is indeed impressive.

The lessons which follow seek to do three things: to establish the fact that totalitarian systems do seek to subordinate all of society to their wills; to explain how such subordination takes place; and finally to reveal why such subordination seems necessary to the state. The lessons which follow are designed to meet these three objectives. They are grouped under four sub-generalizations. Each sub-generalization contributes to an understanding of a specific aspect of the general phenomena.

Sub-Generalization A: *Totalitarian systems attempt—and succeed to a degree—to direct the behavior and thoughts of their citizens by maintaining control over all sources of information.*

The comprehensiveness of totalitarianism in the twentieth century is partly a result of the development of mass communication.

Movies, television, and radio quickly speed information to even the most remote parts of our planet. Whereas people once depended upon receiving news by word of mouth or, for those who could read, by newspapers and magazines, today few individuals are outside earshot of happenings around the globe. The issue today, therefore, is not whether a citizen has access to the news but whether what he hears is accurate and reliable. Totalitarian rulers do not permit their subjects to have access to news which might question the policies of the regime. The deliberate use of propaganda and lies to control the populace has become one of the distinguishing characteristics of totalitarian regimes. The words of Joseph Goebbels, Propaganda Minister in Nazi Germany —"Propaganda made the Third Reich" and "People are more easily taken in by a big lie than a small lie"—reveal how cynically totalitarian leaders have manufactured evidence to control the thoughts and behavior of their subjects.

The lesson which follows should contribute to students' understanding of totalitarian control of information. The lesson is based upon an incident which you can stage in cooperation with four students, a teacher in an adjoining classroom, and the administration. To achieve the intended effect, participants must be carefully briefed in advance and the incident very carefully timed. The account which follows describes how such an "incident" might be created before your class. Let us assume, for purposes of timing the experience, that the class period is one hour in length, extending from 9:00-10:00 A.M. After you have checked attendance, you should have some materials to distribute to the students which will occupy them at their seats for the first 30 minutes of the period. This material is only a decoy, but the students should not know this.

The hypothetical incident:

At 9:10, four boys come in late. One boy, we shall call him John, is one who would never be suspected of fighting, although his clothes are rumpled and his hair is mussed. (It is important that the student who plays "John" be the kind of person least likely to get involved in a brawl.) Let us assume that the other three boys are named Charles, Bob, and Richard.

You: (*After the boys have reached their seats*) Boys, why are you late? (No answer) Boys, I have to have a reason since you are late.

Richard: I stopped to watch a fight outside the building.

You: Fight! I didn't know there was a fight. What about it, class? Was there a fight between periods? (Students will probably indicate that they were unaware of a fight. A few might say there was a fight, either prompted by mischief or a desire to support Richard's story.)

You: Well, Richard. You don't seem to have much support for your fight excuse. If there was a fight, who was fighting?

Richard: I don't want to tell on anyone, but since you asked me, John was one of them. (Some students will laugh if John is not the type of boy who would normally be suspected of fighting.)

John: I was not fighting.

Bob: There's no point lying about it. You were fighting. I saw you.

Charles: John was not fighting. He was with me. He was not in a fight.

You: Wait a minute! There seems to be a strong difference of opinion. Richard and Bob say that John was fighting; John and Charles deny he was fighting. How about it class? Whom do we believe? (Class takes a vote; since John does not appear to be a fighter, most will probably vote that he was not fighting.)

You: I want you boys to stay a moment after class, and we shall get to the bottom of this. We can't take time now to get the truth. (You then tell the class to go on with its work and hand lessons to the four late arrivals.) At 9:15, a teacher from an adjoining classroom comes to the door, speaking only to you but loud enough so the class can hear: There was a fight outside the building between classes. I didn't see who was fighting, but I think some of your boys might have been involved. (The teacher leaves.)

At 9:20, an office girl arrives and informs you that John is wanted in the principal's office. She provides no details explaining why his presence is requested. As soon as John is out of the room, Charles confesses to having been a false witness.

Charles: It appears that John is in trouble. I don't know whether he was fighting or not; I wasn't with him. I lied for him because I could not believe that he had been fighting.

(You take some time to preach about the importance of telling the truth. Students return to their work. At 9:30, they are interrupted by the principal or chief disciplinarian's voice over the public address system.)

Principal: Mr. (You), John will be returning in a few minutes to get his books. He is being sent home for fighting and will not be permitted back into school until we can talk to his parents.

(A few minutes later John returns to the room, looking badly scared and disturbed. He retrieves his books and on his way out of the room, stops at your desk.)

John: Mr. (You), I'm sorry that I lied to you. I was fighting, and I knew I should not have been. I lied to protect myself and to keep from being punished. (John leaves.)

After John has gone, tell the students to put aside their regular work as something rather interesting has taken place and you wish to explore it. Ask the students to take a piece of paper and answer the following questions:

1. Were you at first aware that there had been a fight between classes? Did you see it or hear it before you came to class?
2. Did you believe at first that John had been in a fight?
3. At what point did you decide John had been fighting?
    a. When the boys arrived late?
    b. When you learned there had been a fight?
    c. When you saw John's rumpled clothes?
    d. When Richard said John had been fighting?
    e. When the teacher said there had been a fight and the four boys might be involved?
    f. When the secretary called John to the office?
    g. When Richard confessed that he did not know whether John was fighting or not?
    h. When the principal said John was being sent home for fighting?
    i. When John confessed?
4. If you still do not believe John was fighting, what would it take to convince you?

Ask the students to pass their answers to the students at the front of each row, and let these students read the responses from each paper while the teacher tabulates them on the board. After the results are posted, announce that there had never been a fight and that the whole incident was a hoax. Compare the results posted on the board with the actual facts of the case. Hopefully, for the purposes of this lesson, the majority of students will have been fooled.[14] Ask why they were led to incorrect conclusions. [They were dependent upon false evidence completely in control of the teacher. They are used to acting on evidence and therefore were misled. They moved from a belief there was no fight at all to a belief in a fight and John's participation in it.] How might totalitarian rulers control evidence? What sources of information would have to be controlled? [Books, magazines, films, television, radio, newspapers, billboards and many others.] What is likely to happen if one hears only the opinions and facts supplied by his political leaders? Why would students in a totalitarian state be less likely to have fallen for this incident than you were? [It is clear that citizens under totalitarian rule learn to be critical and skeptical about what they read or hear. Despite this skepticism they are still often misled because there is no other evidence to act upon. Nevertheless, students in a democracy expect to hear the truth and are probably taken in more quickly than those who are used to coping with falsehood.] What would be needed to convince the last holdouts that John had been fighting? Torture, threats, reprisals of various kinds? All of these are available to totalitarian rulers.

The teacher may also wish to take each of the questions asked of the students and point to parallels in totalitarian countries. Rumor, voice of authority, false testimony, confessions—all had their place in this incident as they do in totalitarian regimes. For example, ask students why they did not leave the room to ask other students and teachers about the alleged fight. The students will reply that once class has begun, they are not allowed to leave their rooms and wander around the corridors chatting with students and teachers. In other words, the only information available to the students in the room is that which you choose to make available. Relate this fact to the curbs on travel totalitarian rulers place on their citizens. Why are Russians discouraged from having contacts with Americans? You will also want to discuss the government-controlled press and radio and television programming in totalitarian countries. Mention the purge trials in Nazi

---

[14] When this lesson was tried by the author with a class of seniors, only one student in a class of 30 failed to become convinced that John had been fighting. He said that he would believe John had been fighting only after he had spoken to the other boy who was accused of fighting.

Germany and Soviet Russia and relate them to "the confessions" by "Charles" and "John."

You may wish to ask the students if they feel guilty about having falsely judged John. Would incidents of this kind destroy trust in others? What might distrust of others do to one's ability to hold out against the desires of the regime? Finally, lead the students to state sub-generalization A in their own words.

Sub-Generalization B: *A totalitarian state seeks to force conformity on its citizens and subordinate all human activity to its control.*

In the previous lesson students were confronted with the realities of totalitarianism by being made victims of false testimony and evidence. They were urged to consider how a state might seek to control all sources of information and what the results of such control on citizens might be.

In this lesson students can see how a totalitarian regime seeks to impose conformity, and direct the personal lives of its citizens. The space limitations of this guide do not permit exploration of all the areas of human concern which are affected by totalitarianism. An example from the arts was chosen because the contrast between democratic and totalitarian attitudes towards cultural activities can be observed easily. In democratic countries the artist may be driven only by aesthetic considerations or the moods and experiences he wishes to convey. In totalitarian states, the arts must somehow promote patriotism, glorify the leadership, and advance the political and economic goals of the state. Art for art's sake is not tolerated.

There is yet another way in which the arts provide an apt illustration. We often expect the artist to be a non-conformist, a person who prides himself on his individuality and detachment from mass society. Non-conformists or "deviants" are not popular with totalitarians. Whether the deviant is a member of a specific ethnic group which the regime seeks to extirpate, as with the Jews under Nazi domination, or of a socio-economic class such as the bourgeoisie which the Communists try to eliminate, or simply an individual who wants to hold himself aloof from the mass society, the regime must either absorb or eliminate him. The defendant in the case below was a deviant, according to the Soviet authorities, in several respects: He carried on his activities without the official support of any institution or organization; he criticized the ideology of the regime in his writings; he was not motivated by desires for more material possessions; and he wrote and translated poetry for its own sake, not because the poetry glorified communism, was educational, or readily intelligible to the Soviet public.

It should also be noted that the artist represents a potential threat to a totalitarian regime because of his ability to portray and criticize the society in which he lives. Great artists may have lived on the peripheries of the mass society, but their works have provided succeeding generations with penetrating observations and analyses of their environments. As an individual, the artist can seem dangerous simply because he is or seeks to be autonomous; as an artist, the gifted person can be dangerous if his talents are directed toward the creation of powerfully attractive works which undermine the regime. One can only speculate if Brodsky's trial would have been so widely publicized, if he had been merely an obscure scribbler rather than a poet beginning to enjoy some respect and prestige among other artists and scholars.

SUGGESTED PROCEDURE

The reading is a transcript of the trial of Josef Brodsky, which took place in Leningrad during February and March, 1964. You may wish to duplicate this record and ask students to read it at home in preparation for class discussion. Or, the class could prepare a mock trial based on this material. One student could serve as the judge, another as Brodsky, two others as the prosecuting and defense counsels. While these students remained in the front of the classroom throughout the "trial," other students would come from their seats to serve as witnesses. The witnesses could remain unknown to their fellow classmates until they came forward to testify in order to replicate the conditions in a society where one does not know on whom one can depend. Members of the class who do not have specific roles could be asked to pass judgment on Brodsky at the end of the trial.

Brodsky was found guilty, and was sentenced to five years of hard labor. Despite persistent rumors about his release, it is generally assumed that he is still working as a dung carrier on a state farm near Archangel.

The trial provides a number of topics for discussion. The Soviet Constitution guarantees a "right to work." According to the Court and to the witnesses, how is this right interpreted? What is the purpose of work, according to the State? Why is there some question about Brodsky's working alone? Why should it be important, as far as the State is concerned, that he belong to clubs and organizations recognized by the state? Throughout the trial, the witnesses for the prosecution link Brodsky to other people whom they consider to be undesirable elements in society. What is guilt by association?

After the trial students can be asked to "pass judgment" on Brodsky. How would they treat him if they were Soviet officials? American jurists? Do they think that Brodsky had committed any crimes?

There is also an opportunity to bring out again the role which ideology plays in the totalitarian regime by asking students to compare Brodsky's attitude toward communism with that of the young man considered on pages 58 and 59 of this guide. To what degree are citizens expected to be loyal to the party in power? To the ideology of the State? Do students think that the State demands more or less loyalty from artists and intellectuals? Why? If they had to choose between being a Brodsky or the young Communist, which would students rather be? What personal psychological factors might account for the different attitudes of these young men?

The trial may also be used to form a judgment about the degree of totalitarianism which presently exists in the Soviet Union. While Soviet leaders may aspire to control deviant thought and behavior, Brodsky's testimony as well as that of the defense witnesses suggest that their aspirations have not been totally successful.

Finally, ask students to consider what this trial represents in the broader context of totalitarianism. Students should understand why totalitarian rulers seek to control all aspects of society and thereby approach an understanding of sub-generalization B.

TRIAL OF A YOUNG POET[15]

In February, 1964, the Soviet poet Josef Brodsky was brought to trial. He was accused of being "a work-shy element, a lout, an artful dodger, a man who is spiritually dirty." As you read the record of his trial, consider the following questions:

1. What is Brodsky's crime in the view of the prosecution?
2. Would he be considered a criminal in the United States?
3. How can one be an honest poet in the eyes of the prosecution?
4. Do you consider the trial a fair one with respect to the decree of May 4, 1961?
5. Do you think Brodsky was judged innocent or guilty by the Soviet court? Would the result have been the same in the United States?
6. What does the reading illustrate about the role of the individual in a totalitarian state?

"4 May, 1961

"On the Intensification of the Struggle Against Persons Avoiding Work for the Common Good and Leading an Anti-Social Parasitic Life.

"It is ordered that adult citizens able to work who will not fulfill the most important duty laid down by the Constitution, namely to work honestly according to their abilities, who avoid work for the common good, who profit from gains not arising out of work, from the exploitation of land, automobile vehicles, living-accommodation, or who commit other anti-social acts that enable them to lead parasitic lives, in accordance with the decision of the People's Court of the City District are liable to deportation to places specially selected for the purpose for a period of two to five years and to forced labour in the place of their penal settlement, together with simultaneous seizure of their property not acquired by work.

N. Organov, *President of the Praesidium of the Supreme Soviet of the R.S.F.S.R.*

S. Orlov, *Secretary of the Praesidium of the Supreme Soviet of the R.S.F.S.R.*

---

[15] "Trial of a Young Poet," *Encounter*, London, England Vol. XXII, 3 (September, 1964) 84-91.

"Session of the Court of the Dzerzhinsky District of the City of Leningrad

First hearing of the case against Josef Brodsky
on February 18th, 1964
Presiding Judge: Mrs. Savelya.

Judge: What is your occupation?

Brodsky: I write poems. I translate. I suppose. . . .

Judge: Never mind what you 'suppose.' Stand properly. Don't lean against the wall. Look at the Court. Answer the Court properly. Have you a regular job?

Brodsky: I thought that was a regular job.

Judge: Give a clear answer.

Brodsky: I wrote poems. I thought they would be printed. I suppose. . . .

Judge: We're not interested in what you 'suppose.' Answer why you didn't work.

Brodsky: I did work. I wrote poems. . . .

Judge: Did you learn that?

Brodsky: What?

Judge: To be a poet. You didn't attempt to go to a university, where people are trained . . . where they're taught? . . .

Brodsky: I didn't think . . . I didn't think that could be done by training.

Judge: What by, then?

Brodsky: I thought that . . . by God. . . .

Judge: Have you a request to make of the Court?

Brodsky: I should like to know why I've been arrested.

Judge: That is a question, not a request.

Brodsky: Then I have no request to make.

Judge: Has the defence any questions to ask?

Defence Counsel: Yes. Citizen Brodsky, do you give what you earn to your family?

Brodsky: Yes. . . .

Defence Counsel: You have translated poems for an anthology of Cuban poets?

Brodsky: Yes.

Defence Counsel: I ask the Court to add to the papers of the case the expert opinion of the office of the Translator's Section. A list of the translated poems. Copies of the contracts. And I ask for Citizen Brodsky to be medically examined to ascertain whether his state of health has prevented him from doing regular work. Furthermore, I ask for Citizen Brodsky to be immediately released. I am of the opinion that he has committed no crime and that his arrest is illegal. He has a permanent place of residence and can appear before the Court at any time.

The Court retires for consultation and then reads out the following decision:

To be sent for a Court Psychiatrist's report on the question: Is Brodsky suffering from some psychological illness and does this make it impossible to send Brodsky to forced labour in a remote area? To pass the papers of the case to the Militia to check Brodsky's employment contracts. . . .

Judge: Have you any questions?

Brodsky: I have a request. To be given pen and paper in my cell.

Judge: This request must be addressed to the chief of the Militia.

Brodsky: I asked him and he refused. I ask for pen and paper.

Judge: I shall pass your request on.

Brodsky: Thank you. . . .

Second hearing of the case against Josef Brodsky (Fontanka 22, hall of the Building Workers' Club, on March 13th, 1964).

Announcement:

'LEGAL PROCEEDINGS AGAINST THE WORK-SHY ELEMENT BRODSKY'

The psychiatric report reads: 'Psychopathic character traits observable, but capable of working. Hence measures of an administrative character may be taken.'

The Judge asks Brodsky what requests he has to make to the Court. It emerges that he has not yet seen a copy of the indictment. The hearing is adjourned, and he is taken out so that he can read the indictment. On being brought in again, he declares that several of the poems are not by him. Furthermore, he requests that the journal which he wrote in 1956, when he was sixteen, should not be included among the documents of the case. The journal is not removed. The Judge asks him why he has changed his place of work thirteen times since 1956, and at intervals in between has not worked.

Sorokin (Public Prosecutor): Is it possible to live on the money you earn?

Brodsky: It is possible. Since I have been in prison I have signed a statement every day to say that 40 kopecks [approximately 40 cents] have been spent on me. And I have earned more than 40 kopecks a day.

Sorokin: Don't you need shoes and suits?

Brodsky: I have a suit, an old one, but a suit of sorts. I don't need a second. . . .

Defence Counsel: Have experts expressed approval of your poems?

Brodsky: Yes, I've been printed in the almanac *For the First Time in the Russian Language* and have given readings of translations from the Polish.

Judge (to the Defence Counsel): You are supposed to be asking him what useful work he has done, and you ask him about his readings.

Counsel: His translations are useful work.

Judge: It would be better, Brodsky, if you would explain to the Court why you didn't work during the breaks between jobs.

Brodsky: I wrote poems. I did work.

Judge: But you could have worked at the same time.

Brodsky: I did work. I wrote poems.

Judge: But there are people who work in a factory and write poems. What prevented you from doing that?

Brodsky: But people aren't all the same. Even the colour of their hair, the expression of their faces. . . .

Judge: That's not your discovery. Everyone knows that. It would be better if you explained how you assess your share in our forward movement towards Communism.

Brodsky: The building of Communism—that doesn't only mean standing at the work-bench or ploughing the soil. That also means intellectual work which. . . .

Judge: Never mind the high-sounding words. Tell us how you intend to arrange your working activity in future.

Brodsky: I wanted to write and translate poems. But if that contradicts the general norm, I shall take a fixed job and write poems in spite of it.

Judge Tyagly: In our country everyone works. How were you able to laze about for so long?

Brodsky: You don't look upon my work as work. . . .

The Judge holds out to him the article in the Vecherniy Leningrad *entitled 'A Literary Parasite,' which is about Brodsky. Brodsky declares that the author, Lerner, is lying: his age is given wrongly, the poems are not by him, his supposed friends are people he scarcely knew or did not know at all.*

Judge: Witness Grudinina.

Grudinina: I have been in charge of the work of young poets for more than eleven years. For seven years I was a member of the commission for work with young authors. Now I am in charge of the poets of the higher classes in the Pioneer Palace and the circle of young authors in the Svetlana factory. At the request of the publishing house I have compiled and edited four anthologies of young poets, which comprise more than two hundred new names. In this way I have a practical knowledge of the work of almost all the young poets of the city. Brodsky's work as a beginner is known to me on the basis of his poems from the years '59 and '60. These were not finished poems, but they contained clear ideas and images. I didn't include them in the anthologies, but I considered the author to be talented.[16] . . . As a poetess and literary scholar by training I can confirm that Brodsky's translations are of a high professional quality. Brodsky has a specific talent for the artistic translation of poems such as is not often met with. He gave me a work of 368 lines of verse; moreover, I read 120 lines of poems translated by him and printed in Moscow publications. From personal experience of artistic translation I know that a work of such proportions demands of the author not less than a year and a half of full-time work, to say nothing of the bother connected with the publication of the poems and of the consultations with specialists. As is well known, it is impossible to assess accurately the time required for these troublesome extras. If these translations are valued at even the lowest publisher's rates that I have seen with my own eyes, Brodsky has already earned 350 roubles, [approximately 385 dollars] and the question is when everything he has done will be printed in full. . . . Brodsky lives in a very humble style, goes without clothes and amusements, and spends the greater part of his time at his desk. The money he receives from his work, he gives to his family. . . .

---

[16] *Ed. Note:* Almost nothing of Brodsky's own verse has been published in Russia, although many poems have been circulating in mimeographed form and have made his reputation. "I first heard his name," the American critic Andrew Field writes, "when the elderly Anna Akhmatova, Russia's greatest living poet, praised his poetry in a conversation on the work of the younger generation, adding 'that might be because he writes like me though'. . . . As a poet Brodsky does show the strong influence of Akhmatova, and also of the famous Russian poet Osip Mandelstam. His poems are unassertive and deceptively conversational in style; their aim is frequently to convey the strangeness and awkwardness of life in the simplest possible manner. . . ." These are the concluding lines of Brodsky's poem entitled "Monument to Pushkin":

> An empty street.
> And a monument to a poet.
> An empty street.
> And the singing of the storm.
> And a head
> bent down in tiredness.
>
> . . . On such a night
> to toss about in bed
> is pleasanter,
>   than to stand
> on pedestals.

Judge Lebedeva: Can a foreign language be learnt by studying on one's own?

Grudinina: I have learnt two languages on my own, in addition to those which I learnt at the university. . . .

Judge: But why does he work in isolation? Why doesn't he belong to any literary societies?

Grudinina: In 1958 he asked to join my literary association. But I had heard of him as being a hysterical boy and didn't accept him; I rejected him personally. That was my mistake, and I regret it very much. Now I would very willingly accept him into my association and work with him, if he wants me to. . . .

Counsel: One other thing I wanted to ask you, witness. . . . Brodsky's production for 1963 is as follows: poems in the book *Dawn over Cuba;* translations of poems by Galczynski (of course, not published yet); poems in the book *Yugoslav Poets;* gaucho songs and publications in *Kostyor.* Can that be regarded as serious work?

Grudinina: Yes, without a doubt. This is a year filled with work. But this work cannot bring in any money for at least a few years. It is wrong to judge the value of a young author's work by the level of the fees he is at present receiving. A young author may fail at first; new time-consuming work may be needed. There is a joke that says: the difference between a work-shy element and a young poet is that the work-shy element doesn't work, but eats —while the young poet works, but doesn't eat.

Judge: We object to that statement. In our country everyone receives the appropriate reward for his work, therefore it is impossible for anyone to have done a great deal of work and received little money. You say that in our country where so much sympathy is shown for young poets, you say they go hungry. Why did you say young poets don't eat?

Grudinina: I didn't put it like that. I pointed out that it is a joke in which there is some truth. The income of young poets is very irregular.

Judge: Well, that depends upon them. You didn't have to tell us that. All right, you have explained that you were speaking in jest. We accept your explanation.

A new witness is called, Yefim Grigorievich Etkind.

Judge: Give us your pass, since your name is pronounced somehow unclearly. Etkind . . . Yefim Gershovich. . . . We are listening to you.

Etkind (Member of the Association of Soviet Writers, lecturer at the Herzen Institute): In conformity with the nature of my social and literary work, which is connected with the training of be-

ginner translators, I often have occasion to read or hear translations by young men of letters. About a year ago I had an opportunity of seeing works by Brodsky. They were translations
of poems by the outstanding Polish lyric poet Galczynski, few
of whose poems have been translated into our language. The
clarity of the poetic phraseology, the music of his language, the
passion and energy of the poems made a strong impression on
me. I was also surprised by the fact that Brodsky had learned
the Polish language on his own, without any help from others.
. . . I have had many conversations with Brodsky and been
surprised by his knowledge in the field of American, English,
and Polish literature. The translation of poems is extraordinarily
hard work that demands tenacious diligence, knowledge, and
talent. . . .

Judge: But why doesn't he belong to any collective?

Etkind: He comes to our translator's seminars. . . .

Smirnov (*Chief of the 'House of Defence,' witness for the prosecution*):
I am not personally acquainted with Brodsky, but I wish to say
that if all citizens had the same attitude as Brodsky towards the
accumulation of material values, Communism would not be built
for a long time. Intelligence is a dangerous weapon for those
who possess it. Everyone has said that he is intelligent and
almost a genius. But no one has said what kind of person he is.
He grew up in a family belonging to the intelligentsia, but he
only had seven years' schooling. Let those present say whether
they would like to have a son who only went to elementary
school. He didn't go into the army because he was the sole support of his family. But what a support! They say he is a gifted
translator, but why doesn't anyone say what muddled ideas he
has in his head? And his anti-Soviet verses? . . .

Brodsky: When I was released as the sole support of my family, my
father was ill after a heart attack, but I was working and earn-
ing money. And then I was ill. How do you come to know me
so that you can talk about me like that?

Smirnov: I have looked at your personal journal.

Brodsky: By what right?

Judge: I shall not permit that question.

Smirnov: I have read poems of his.

Counsel: There were poems among the documents that are not by
Brodsky. How do you know that the poems you read were
really his poems? Because you are speaking of unpublished
poems.

Smirnov: I know, and that's enough! . . .

Denisov (plumber from UNR-20): I am not personally acquainted with Brodsky. I only know him from the statements published in our Press. I speak as a citizen and a representative of the public. After the statements in the papers I was indignant about Brodsky's work. I wanted to get to know his books. I went to the library—there are no books by him. I asked acquaintances if they knew someone of that name. No, they didn't know him. I'm a worker. In all my life I have only changed my place of work twice. And Brodsky? I'm not satisfied with Brodsky's statement that he has mastered many trades. You can't learn one single trade in such a short time. People say Brodsky is a poet or something. Why wasn't he a member of any association? Doesn't he agree with dialectical materialism? Engel says that work has made man. But Brodsky isn't satisfied with this formulation. He is of a different opinion. Perhaps he is very gifted, but why doesn't he find his way into our literature? Why doesn't he work? I would like to state that his activities don't satisfy me as a worker.

Judge: Witness Nikolaiev.

Nikolaiev (*Pensioner*): I am not personally acquainted with Brodsky. I should like to say that I have known for the last three years of the pernicious influence which he exercises on his contemporaries. I am a father and I have been convinced by my own experience of how hard it is to have a son who doesn't work. I have more than once seen poems of Brodsky's in my son's possession. One poem in 42 sections and also individual poems. I know Brodsky from the Umansky case. There is a proverb: 'Tell me who your friends are. . . .' I knew Umansky personally. He was a bitter enemy of the Soviet Union. My son also told me that he considers himself a genius. Like Brodsky, he won't work. People like Brodsky and Umansky have a pernicious influence on their contemporaries. . . .

Counsel: Why do you think it was Brodsky and not Umansky who had a pernicious influence on your son?

Nikolaiev: I mean Brodsky and his sort. Brodsky has written shameful and anti-Soviet poems.

Brodsky: Name my anti-Soviet poems. Repeat one single line.

Judge: I shall not permit quotations.

Brodsky: But I want to know what poems he is talking about. Perhaps they're not by me. . . .

Romashova (*Teacher of Marxism-Leninism at the Mukhina Educational Institute*): I don't know Brodsky personally. But his so-called activity is known to me. Pushkin said that talent is above all hard work. And Brodsky? Has he by any chance tried, has he worked, to make his poems intelligible to the people? I'm surprised that my colleagues put such a halo round him. Only in the Soviet Union is it possible for a Court to speak so benevolently with a poet, to advise him in such a comradely way to learn. As secretary of the Party organisation of the Mukhina Educational Institute I can say that he has a bad influence on youth.

Counsel: Have you ever seen Brodsky?

Romashova: Never. But Brodsky's so-called activity allows me to form an opinion of him. . . .

Counsel: And you yourself know Brodsky's poems?

Romashova: I know them. They're horrible. I consider it impossible to repeat them. They're horrible.

Judge: Witness Admoni. If possible, your pass, since the name is unusual.

Admoni (Professor at the Herzen Institute, linguist, literary scholar, translator): When I learnt that Brodsky had been summoned to appear before the Court on a charge of being work-shy I felt it my duty to state my own opinion before the Court. I believe I am justified in doing so because I have been working with young people for thirty years as a university teacher, and because I have long been occupied with translations. I scarcely know Josef Brodsky. . . . For over a year, however, I have been following his work as a translator with great attention—on the basis of his appearances at the translators' evenings and on the basis of publications. And on the basis of these translations of Galczynski, Fernandez, and others I can say with complete responsibility that they demanded exceptionally hard work from their author. They bear witness to great skill and culture on the part of the translator. . . . When I learnt to-day—for the first time —that he had only had seven years of schooling, it became clear to me that he must have done a truly gigantic amount of work in order to have acquired the skill and culture that he possesses to-day. Mayakovsky's comment on the work of the poet also applies to the translator of poetry: 'For the sake of a single word you laboriously shift a thousand tons of ore-bearing rock. . . .' . . . It is impossible to accuse a man who works like Brodsky of being work-shy—a man who works hard and much, does not think of big earnings, is content with the absolute minimum necessities of life in order to perfect himself in his art and to produce translations of high artistic quality. . . .

Judge: Citizen Brodsky, you have only occasionally worked. Why?

Brodsky: I have already said that I have worked all the time. In a fixed job and then I wrote poems. That's work—writing poems.

Judge: But you've earned very little.

Sorokin (Public Prosecutor): Our great nation is building Communism. In Soviet man an outstanding characteristic is developing: joy in socially useful work. Only the society in which there is no idleness flourishes. Brodsky is far removed from patriotism. He has forgotten the most important principle: he who does not work shall not eat. But Brodsky has been leading the life of a work-shy element for many years. In 1956 he left school and entered a factory. He was fifteen at the time. He was dismissed the same year. (*Repeats the list of his places of employment and declares the breaks between regular employment to have been periods of idleness.*) We have checked and discovered that for one piece of work Brodsky received only 37 roubles, whereas he said he received 150.

Brodsky: That's an advance. That's only an advance! A part of what I'm to get later.

Judge: Silence, Brodsky.

Sorokin: Where Brodsky worked he shocked everyone by his lack of discipline and dislike of work. The article in *Vecherniy Leningrad* met with great approval. A particularly large number of letters were received from young people. They sharply condemned Brodsky's behaviour. (*Reads letters.*) The young are of the opinion that there is no place for him in Leningrad, that he must be severely punished. He lacks all understanding for conscience and duty. Everyone regards it as a joy to serve in the army. But he dodged it. Brodsky's father sent his son to be examined at the out-patient clinic, and he brought from there a certificate which a credulous military commission accepted. . . . He belonged to the company of those who greeted the word 'work' with Satanic laughter and listened with reverence to their 'leader' Umansky. Brodsky is allied to him by his hatred of work and of Soviet literature. Pornographic words and ideas enjoy special success here. . . . Brodsky is defended by artful dodgers, work-shy elements, woodlice, and beetles. Brodsky isn't a poet, but a man who tries to write puny verses. He has forgotten that in our country man must work, must create values: jobs or bread or poems. We must compel Brodsky to do forced labour. We must banish him from our heroic city. . . . Why have people defended a man who hates our fatherland? We must scrutinise the moral countenance of those who have defended him. . . . In his journals there is a note: 'I have been thinking for a long time of crossing the red frontier. . . .' And he also wrote: 'The Town Hall in Stockholm inspires more respect in me than the Kremlin in Prague. . . .' He called Marx: 'An old greedy-guts framed by a wreath of fir-cones.' In a letter he wrote: 'I should like to spit on Moscow.' That's what Brodsky is worth and all who defend him."

The record of the defence counsel's summing-up is missing. Its conclusions were: Brodsky's guilt has not been proved; Brodsky is not a work-shy element, therefore 'means of administrative influence' cannot be applied to him. The importance of the decree of May 4th is very great; it is a weapon for ridding the city of real work-shy elements and parasites. Its groundless application discredits the purpose of the degree. The decision of the Supreme Court of the Soviet Union of March 10th, 1963, makes it the duty of the Court to adopt a critical attitude towards the evidence submitted, not to allow a verdict against those who are working, and to respect the right of the accused to acquaint themselves with the documents of the case and to submit evidence of their innocence. Brodsky was illegally held in custody from February 13th, 1964, and deprived of the possibility of presenting a number of pieces of evidence. But even the evidence submitted is sufficient for the conclusion that Brodsky is not a work-shy element.
(The Court retires for consultation.)

Sub-Generalization C: *Totalitarian regimes will use any technique —physical or psychological—to achieve absolute control over society.*

When reason and persuasion fail to move the populace along paths desired by the regime, totalitarian leaders resort to the use of terror. Terror does not have to be directed at real enemies; in fact, confusion about the reasons for arrests and execution may cause people to be even more docile and cooperative than they would be if they were aware of the victims' crimes.

For totalitarian leaders terror serves at least three purposes: It eliminates the real or imagined enemies of the state; it demonstrates the power and authority of the state; and it frightens potential opposition into silence and conformity.

In the following reading, a Chinese refugee describes an incident in which terror was directed against an identified enemy of the state. As a member of the landlord class, the old man was an enemy of the Chinese Communists. Considerable uncertainty, however, surrounded the "crime" of which he was accused and for which he was killed. This reading also illustrates the way in which terror spreads fear and induces conformity. Liu did not know whether or not it would be a "crime" if he did not participate in the old man's death. Public punishment, the fear of not knowing who would be next and why, uncertainty about who might accuse a person of an actual or fabricated crime, and the demonstrated power of the regime are all combined in this episode. (In contrast to the Brodsky trial, in this trial terror was the technique and elimination of the deviant rather than his reform was the goal.)

Suggested Procedure

You may wish to mimeograph this report of the landlord's trial and assign it as homework. Indicate that the questions preceding the reading will form the basis of class discussion.

When class begins, first make certain that the students understand the main points of the reading. When did the trial take place? Why were landlords tried? By what authority were such trials held?

Next, you will want students to understand the implications of the landlord's trial. Ask them to compare the landlord's trial with the Brodsky trial. For example, students should recognize that the use of terror was a significant factor in the village trial and "due process of law" was largely ignored. And, while the accused was charged with a specific crime, Liu believed that his principal guilt, so far as the judges were concerned, arose from his being a landlord. How was Liu forced to take part in the trial? Did he act from belief, persuasion, fear or a combination of emotions?

Ask students if they can think of other examples in history when entire social classes or religious and ethnic groups have been executed. They will recall the plight of the early Christians in Rome, the aristocracy in France during the French Revolution, the Jews under Nazi rule, and many of the kulaks in the Soviet Union. What safeguards do we have against such miscarriages of justice in the United States? Have certain groups or classes in our own country at times been the victims of established authority?

Finally, your students have had an opportunity to observe three techniques which totalitarian leaders use to dominate various facets of their societies: control of sources of information, legal process, and terror. Encourage students to pull together what they have learned from these three lessons in order to recognize that totalitarian leaders seek to control all aspects of society and they do so through a variety of techniques.

A VILLAGE TRIAL[17]

In 1949 when the Chinese Communists came to power, they began immediately to solidify their hold over the country. Real or imagined enemies of the new regime were hunted down and punished. Perhaps several million people were executed during the initial years of the Communist regime.

One of the methods used by the Communists to destroy all opposition to their power was to hold village trials. These trials were intended to be a kind of "settling of accounts"—that is, paying back past grievances suffered by peasants from wealthy and more powerful landlords. The description you are about to read is an authentic account of such a trial. It is related by a Chinese craftsman who actually participated in this trial before fleeing from the Mainland in 1951.

As you read, keep in mind the following questions:
1. Why did the Communists wish to "try" the landlord?
2. Was the landlord's trial similar to that awarded Brodsky? Was there any doubt of the landlord's guilt in the eyes of the court?
3. What kind of evidence was accepted?
4. Was the landlord tried for his individual crime or because he was the member of an outlawed social class?
5. What effect did the trial have on the observers?
6. Why did the Communists make an example of the landlord rather than give him a private trial and execution?
7. What purposes other than the elimination of the landlord could the Communists have had in mind by conducting a trial in this manner?

---

[17] Robert Burton. "A Chinese Craftsman Under Three Regimes." American Universities Field Staff Report, East Asia Series: Vol. VIII, No. 1 [January, 1960] 36-41. In this same report Liu also describes economic measures which the Farmers' Association used to control peasants as well as landlords (pp. 34-36). Students who wish to explore futher the purposes and methods of terror in a totalitarian regime may wish to read *The Diary of a Young Girl*, written by Anne Frank, a thirteen-year old Jewish girl, whose family perished under the Nazis.

"Although the Communists seldom bothered the poorer farmers in the beginning, they went fiercely after the landlords. The landlords had lived extravagantly at the expense of the people in the past, the Communists said, and now they must pay for it—there must be a settling of accounts. This was not a part of land reform, which came much later. . . .

"Naturally, I was assured at the meetings that landlords were enemies of the people. Well, you know, some of the big landlords really were bad. The farmers of Yen Ping despised some of them. These were the greedy men who lent money at fantastic interest to peasants who had to have the money to tide them over until harvest time; maybe they forced the peasants even deeper into debt by renting out land at high rates—things like that. . . . In any case, when the Communists preached their hatred of landlords, a lot of peasants knew what they were talking about. And when, at a huge public meeting, a terrified landlord, his hands and feet tied with rope, was put on show to cringe before the peasants and they were asked what should be done, sometimes they shouted 'kill him, kill him' because they meant it. But not all landlords were bad, and we knew that. They weren't all greedy. In time of need, you could turn to some of them for a loan and know that they would charge you only a fair interest—or, sometimes, no interest. Some of them were kindly. The Communists went too far in their handling of landlords—much too far.

"At first I paid no attention to the settling of accounts meetings. They were no business of mine. Sometimes a landlord was killed at a meeting, sometimes one was tortured, and sometimes one was declared to be sort of outcast and left to live as best he could until land reform came along. The meetings seemed to be meant to terrify the landlord into admitting every particle of wealth he owned, into confessing the foulness of his past crimes against the people, into begging for mercy. . . .

"But, as I said, sometimes the Communists did not destroy the bad landlords only. Sometimes they went after the good landlords even more furiously because they were afraid of the good landlords' influence. The first settling of accounts meeting I attended was like that. I knew the old gentleman who was on trial fairly well. He lived in the village next to ours. He had returned there to die after spending most of his life in America, where he had worked hard and saved his money so that he could spend a peaceful old age back in his native village. . . . He came back to the village after the Japanese war, and bought a nice piece of land, and built a good house on it. There he quietly spent his fading years, raising pigs and chickens and enjoying the comforts he had sacrificed his younger years to earn. I guess he must have been more than seventy years old. Everyone liked him. He had a reputation for generosity, and most people could turn to him when they needed help. My old uncle sometimes borrowed money from him. The two of them got along quite well, and the old man did not charge my uncle any interest. He was the kind of person who wanted nothing but to enjoy the years that were left to him. He no longer cared about making money.

"After liberation, the Communists taxed him dry. When he could no longer pay the taxes, they branded him a despot and hurled all sorts of ridiculous charges against him. He had adopted a daughter in his old age, for example. She had died a couple of years earlier of some serious disease. The old man had called in a doctor all the way from Canton, but apparently nothing could have saved her life. Yet the Communists claimed he had poisoned the girl after making her pregnant. . . .

"In the case of the old man, he treated the girl like a blood daughter. He had no grandchildren at home, and she filled that need in him. She was lucky to find such a home. I can't believe that he poisoned her, or that he made her pregnant. He was more than seventy years old, after all. Nevertheless, the Communists wanted to destroy him, and they succeeded.

"His trial—his settling of accounts—was carefully prepared by the Farmers' Association. They made it a big thing. Printed circulars about it were sent to all the surrounding villages. The circular explained the man's crimes and ordered each family to send a representative to the meeting. My old uncle was the senior member in our family, but he absolutely refused to go. He still owed the old man some money, and was fond of him. In the end, I went as our representative. . . .

"When I reached the empty market square of the old man's village, I saw a low, rough platform which had been built there especially for the occasion. In front of it was a row of high-backed chairs behind a long wooden table. This was where the judges were to sit. They all turned out to be members of the Farmers' Association. . . . After a while, a crowd of about 300 shabby-looking farmers like myself filled up the square. We squatted around the platform and waited for the trial to begin. Members of the People's Militia stood here and there about the square and on the platform—the type of people who had entered Canton before the Communist regulars arrived, except that now they had proper uniforms and standard rifles. The judges came out and sat self-consciously in their chairs. Finally, the old man was dragged roughly up onto the platform, were he was made to kneel, with his head bowed before the people. . . . He was a skeleton. His face was the color of death. His eyes were lifeless. He stumbled pitifully when he tried to walk. The stringy beard that had been his pride was all matted together, and so was the hair on his head. Most of the people were as startled as I was. You could hear a low murmur from them. It was a murmur of sympathy, but I am sure the old man was too far gone to realize that.

"One of the judges, sounding full of anger, read off the old man's crimes. He had bought the helpless girl in order to sleep with her. When she became pregnant, he had poisoned her, because he was too miserly to support the off-spring. A poor peasant, in desperate need of money, had begged the old man for a loan. Although the old man knew that his refusal would mean starvation for the peasant's family, he had laughed in the peasant's face and turned him away. The old man was a counterrevolutionary agent of the imperialist United States, where his counterrevolutionary agent sons lived. He sent intelligence reports to them regularly through the mails. The terrible charges went on and on.

"When the judge finished reading the charges, people popped up to shout accusations at the old man. The mother of the dead girl stood up, wild-eyed. The old man had murdered her daughter, she shrieked. She began raving, and I couldn't make out what she was saying. Then she rushed at the platform, and spit at the old man, and struggled fiercely to break away from those who held her back to kick him. 'Kill him,' she kept screaming. 'Kill him.'

I don't know who the woman was. Maybe she believed what she was shouting. It wouldn't have been the first time such a thing had happened to a peasant's daughter. Maybe she felt guilty about having sold her daughter, and was trying to make up for it. I don't know. The old man just kneeled there, not showing any emotion at all, not even giving any sign whether or not he heard her.

"Then a man jumped up, his arms waving, and shouted that his family nearly died of starvation because the wealthy old man wouldn't help him. I knew this man. There is one in every village. They can't hold a job, and they won't do the heavy work of farming. They just sit around the wine shops cadging drinks and grinding their teeth in rage because they aren't appreciated. When hard times come, they still sit around the wine shops, expecting someone else to look after their families. Many times the old man gave this fellow money. But there came a time when the old man wouldn't give him any more, because the money never reached the man's family; it was spent on wine. This fellow had become wonderfully progressive since the Communists came into power. I don't think the Communists really trusted him, but they found him useful, and he liked anybody who thought he was useful.

"And so the settling of accounts went on. A shouting, red-faced youngster from the Youth Corps told of seeing the old man write intelligence reports which were sent by mail to America. These, I suppose, were letters to his sons about the village. I squatted there silently, as did the other farmers.

"When all the accusations had been made, a judge, his voice choking with outrage, recited them once more. Then he demanded our verdict. It was up to us, he said, to decide the fate of this vile enemy of the people. Nobody said anything. We just squatted there. Finally, the mother of the dead girl shouted: 'He deserves to be tortured and killed.' Still we were silent. A young student from the city who was there (what did he know about it?) shouted 'Kill him.' There was another long silence. Finally, the judge who had called for a verdict announced: 'It is the will of the people that he be tortured and killed.'

"Some militiamen jerked the fragile old man to his feet and threw him off the platform. Then they wrenched him to his feet again. Other militiamen scattered broken bottles on the ground before him. Cursing him, the militiamen tore off his clothes, except for his underpants, and flung him forward on the jagged glass, where he collapsed, limp. They rolled him back and forth over the glass until his body seemed to ooze blood all over. He moaned a little, and quivered, but that was all. We squatted and watched. There was nothing we could do. All the time the Communists were shouting that this was what the people did to their enemies, and the dead girl's mother kept spitting at the old man and screaming that he should be rolled harder over the glass.

"Then they yanked him up off the glass and made him kneel on the ground. Everybody in the crowd was ordered to beat him three times across the back with a bamboo stake. So we lined up to beat the suffering old man. I didn't want to beat him. The whole business made me sick. But what was I to do? If you didn't beat him as hard as you could, the Communists made you keep on beating him until they were sure that you were really putting your back into it. The old man began screaming in a horrible, high-pitched voice. Every time he opened his mouth to scream, the Communists dashed night soil from a pail into it. They poured it over his head, too. Sometimes they would jerk his head back by the hair and force his mouth open by pulling his beard and pour more night soil into his mouth. And all the time, people were beating him, and he was bleeding all over. Thirty people must have been ahead of me in the line. I prayed that one of them would kill him before my turn came. And then I was at the head of the line, and the bamboo stake was in my hand, and the hard eyes of the Communists were on me, and I hit the withered, stinking old man three times as hard as I could. I think I was hoping to kill him, to bring it all to an end. But I must admit that I was afraid to do anything but hit him hard, too. The Communists were looking for people who sympathized with the old man. I didn't want them to start watching me. I couldn't look at the old man when I hit him. I closed my eyes. Then I had to join the others and watch. Everybody had to watch. The old man kept collapsing, and vomiting blood, and finally they had to hold him up by his hair. After about 40 people had beaten him, he slumped over, dead.

"Then someone from the Farmers' Association talked about what happened to enemies of the people. The people had risen, and their enemies would be stamped out without mercy!

"The filthy corpse, covered with its mixture of blood and night soil, was left where it lay in the hot sun for two days. Nobody was allowed to touch it. Finally, I think, the old man's relatives reached an agreement with the Farmers' Association, and the body was buried in the poorest way possible—without a coffin.

"I saw other public trials. They were not all like this one. But many of them were just as bad."

Sub-Generalization D: *Mass manipulation, subordination of the individual and group association, and the use of terror are all means toward an end. In the view of a totalitarian ruler any means can be justified if it moves society closer toward the professed goals.*

From previous lessons in this guide—especially the skit on the Communist Party, the letter from the young American Communist, and the selection from *Animal Farm*—students have begun to see that totalitarian leaders have goals toward which they direct the energies of those they rule. The achievement of their goals have often been purchased at a tremendous cost in human suffering.

This section is concerned with the justification for mass manipulation through physical and psychological techniques. The "communications" incident staged in class, the trial of Brodsky, and the report of the landlord's public confession and punishment, all raise questions about the relationship between ends and means. Totalitarian leaders operate on the principle that their goals—ideological and economic—justify the means they use to attain those goals.

SUGGESTED PROCEDURE

Since this reading is brief, students may be asked to read it either as a homework or as an in-class assignment. After they have finished their reading, ask them to consider the problem of "ends" and "means" described in the selection. What was the over-riding goal of the Soviet regime during the 1930's? To an-swer this question, refer students to the statement by Stalin used in the lesson on values. In this statement on pages 14 and 15, Stalin makes clear that all the energies of Soviet citizens should be directed toward the rapid industrialization of the country. Other Soviet goals were subordinated to this major one. The tech-niques adopted—some of which are suggested by Rubashov in the following reading—were chosen because they contributed to the rapid industrialization of Russia.

Students should be asked to judge the consequences of Soviet policies. Suppose they had been Soviet leaders in the 1930's; sup-pose also that Stalin's appraisal of the Soviet dilemma was accu-rate: "We are fifty or a hundred years behind the advanced coun-tries. We must make good this distance in ten years. Either we do it, or we shall be crushed." Given these assumptions, would your students have acted as Stalin did? You might point out that Stalin gave this speech in 1931. Ten years later, when Germany attacked the Soviet Union, the Russians absorbed the blow and later drove the invader from their territory. By 1945, the USSR was second only to the United States in national power.

What were the consequences of Stalin's decision to industrialize rapidly? Rubashov suggests some of the consequences. It is clear that the decision for rapid industrialization contributed to, if not required, the development of totalitarianism in Russia. Yet the same decision made possible the successful defense of the nation.

Since American students are unlikely to share Stalin's enthusi-asm for rapid industrialization, they will probably conclude that the cost of human suffering was too great to be justified by that goal. This conclusion may be based upon their belief that the ends do not justify the means, or it may simply reveal that they do not place sufficient value on Stalin's goal.

To test this latter possibility, ask the students if they can think of any goal that is so worthy or noble that it might justify any means to secure its achievement. For example, does the goal of eliminating communism both at home and abroad justify the use of any technique? What methods are permissible to resist com-munism abroad? What means are justified to uncover subversion within the United States?

Some individuals and groups in the United States believe that the elimination of communism is so important to this nation that almost any means can be justified. While professing a desire to further individual freedom, such individuals and groups often behave in totalitarian-like ways. In attempting to lead the fight against specific totalitarian movements which they oppose, they may in turn urge the acceptance of totalitarian behavior and attitudes by Americans. You may wish to have students consider the dangers such groups pose to democratic systems and to individual freedom.[18]

Finally, students should be led to a verbalization of the generalization which opened this lesson. In reaching this generalization, they will have wrestled with the problem of ends and means, dramatically illustrated in *Darkness at Noon*. They should also have begun to understand that willingness to use any technique to achieve a given goal is not limited to totalitarian leaders; certain individuals and groups in democratic societies may be equally zealous. What such individuals and groups lack are the immense power and range of techniques available to the leaders of totalitarian states.

DARKNESS AT NOON[19]

In *Darkness at Noon*, Arthur Koestler recreates the atmosphere of the Moscow purges of 1936-38. The central figure in this novel, Rubashov, is a middle-aged Bolshevik who has fallen from the leader's favor and has been imprisoned by the police. The following excerpt comes from a dialogue between Rubashov and his interrogator, Ivanov. Ivanov, speaking for the regime, presents a classic argument of totalitarian systems that ends justify the means. While reading this passage, you should consider the following questions:

---

[18] Chapter III, "Suggestions for Further Reading," lists a few books which are useful to teachers who wish to consider the threats posed by totalitarians within the United States.

[19] Reprinted with permission of The Macmillan Company from *Darkness at Noon* by Arthur Koestler. Copyright 1941 by The Macmillan Company. Pp. 155-162.

1. What arguments does Ivanov offer to justify restrictions on individual freedom and the use of terror?
2. What is meant by the term "the ends justifies the means"? What examples of this philosophy are contained in the reading?
3. How does Ivanov's philosophy compare to the underlying ideals of democracy?

" 'Really,' said Ivanov. . . . 'Consider a moment what this humanitarian fog-philosophy would lead to, if we were to take it literally; if we were to stick to the precept that the individual is sacrosanct, and that we must not treat human lives according to the rules of arithmetic. That would mean that a battalion commander may not sacrifice a patroling party to save the regiment. That we may not sacrifice fools like Bogrov and must risk our coastal towns being shot to pieces in a couple of years. . . .'

Rubashov shook his head:

'Your examples are all drawn from war—that is, from abnormal circumstances.'

'Since the invention of the steam engine,' replied Ivanov, 'the world has been permanently in an abnormal state; the wars and revolutions are just the visible expressions of this state. . . . The principle that the end justifies the means is and remains the only rule of political ethics; anything else is just vague chatter and melts away between one's fingers. . . .' . . .

'I don't approve of mixing ideologies,' Ivanov continued. 'There are only two conceptions of human ethics, and they are at opposite poles. One of them is Christian and humane, declares the individual to be sacrosanct, and asserts that the rules of arithmetic are not to be applied to human units. The other starts from the basic principle that a collective aim justifies all means, and not only allows, but demands, that the individual should in every way be subordinated and sacrificed to the community—which may dispose of it as an experimentation rabbit or a sacrificial lamb. The first conception could be called antivivisection morality; the second, vivisection morality. Humbugs and dilettantes have always tried to mix the two conceptions; in practice, it is impossible. Whoever is burdened with power and responsibility finds out on the first occasion that he has to choose; and he is fatally driven to the second alternative. Do you know, since the establishment of Christianity as a state religion, a single example of a state which really followed a Christian policy? You can't point out one. In times of need—and politics are chronically in a time of need—the rulers were always able to evoke "exceptional circumstances," which demanded exceptional measures of defense. Since the existence of nations and classes they live in a permanent state of mutual self-defense, which forces them to defer to another time the putting into practice of humanism. . . .' . . .

'Yes,' said Rubashov. . . . 'in the interests of a just distribution of land we deliberately let die of starvation about five million farmers and their families in one year. . . . in the liberation of human beings from the shackles of industrial exploitation . . . we sent about ten million people to do forced labor in the Arctic regions and the jungles of the East, under conditions similar to those of antique galley slaves. . . . to settle a difference of opinion, we know only one argument: death, whether it is a matter of submarines, manure, or the Party line to be followed in Indo-China. Our engineers work with the constant knowledge that an error in calculation may take them to prison or the scaffold; the higher officials in our administration ruin and destroy their subordinates because they know that they will be held responsible for the slightest slip and be destroyed themselves; our poets settle discussions on questions of style by denunciations to the Secret Police, because the expressionists consider the naturalistic style counter-revolutionary, and *vice versa*. Acting consequentially in the interests of the coming generations we have laid such terrible privations on the present one that its average length of life is shortened by a quarter. . . . Our press and our schools cultivate chauvinism, militarism, dogmatism, conformism, and ignorance. The arbitrary power of the government is unlimited, and unexampled in history; freedom of the press, of opinion, and of movement are as thoroughly exterminated as though the proclamation of the Rights of Man had never been. We have built up the most gigantic police apparatus, with informers made a national institution, and with the most refined scientific system of physical and mental torture. We whip the groaning masses of the country toward a theoretical future happiness, which only we can see. . . .

'Well, and what of it?' said Ivanov happily. 'Don't you find it wonderful? Has anything more wonderful ever happened in history? We are tearing the old skin off mankind and giving it a new one. That is not an occupation for people with weak nerves; but there was once a time when it filled you with enthusiasm. What has so changed you that you are now as pernickety as an old maid?'. . .

'For a man with your past,' Ivanov went on, 'this sudden revulsion against experimenting is rather naive. Every year several million people are killed quite pointlessly by epidemics and other natural catastrophes. And we should shrink from sacrificing a few hundred thousand for the most promising experiment in history? Not to mention the legions of those who die of undernourishment and tuberculosis in coal and quicksilver mines, rice fields, and cotton plantations. No one takes any notice of them; nobody asks why or what for; but if here we shoot a few thousand objectively harmful people, the humanitarians all over the world foam at the mouth. Yes, we liquidated the parasitic part of the peasantry and let it die of starvation. It was a surgical operation which had to be done once and for all; but in the good old days before the Revolution just as many died in any dry year—only senselessly and pointlessly. The victims of the Yellow River floods in China amount sometimes to hundreds of thousands. Nature is generous in her senseless experiments on mankind. Why should mankind not have the right to experiment on itself?'

He paused; Rubashov did not answer. He went on:

'Have you ever read brochures of an antivivisectionist society? They are shattering and heartbreaking; when one reads how some poor cur which has had its liver cut out whines and licks his tormentor's hands, one is just as nauseated as you were tonight. But if these people had their say, we would have no serums against cholera, typhoid, or diphtheria. . . .' "

OUTLINE OF LESSON PLAN

Sub-Generalization A:

Four boys, a teacher and an administrator are briefed on the incident to be staged before the class.

Stage the incident; ask students the questions on page 63.

Ask the students why they were misled by the incident.

Lead students to consider how and why totalitarian rulers seek to control all sources of information, drawing parallels to the incident whenever possible.

Formulate the generalization.

Estimated time for this lesson: one day

Sub-Generalization B:

Give students the reading of the Brodsky trial to read at home or stage it as a mock trial before the class.

Ask students to define Brodsky's crime and to speculate about his guilt or innocence.

What does the Brodsky trial demonstrate about the aspirations of totalitarian rulers?

What does the trial reveal about the degree of totalitarianism existing today in the USSR?

Verbalize the generalization.

Estimated time required for this lesson: one or two days

Sub-Generalization C:

Assign "A Village Trial" to be read at home.

Establish the principal facts in the reading.

Compare the landlord trial to the Brodsky trial.

Discuss the functions of terror in a totalitarian state.

Draw comparisons to other occasions in history when regimes have sought to eliminate despised classes or groups.

Lead students to verbalize the generalization.

Estimated time required for this lesson: one day

Sub-Generalization D:

Assign *Darkness at Noon* to be read, either in class or at home.

Refer to Stalin's value statement on pages 14-15.

Ask students to define the major Soviet goal in the 1930's.

Discuss consequences arising from the means adopted to achieve this goal.

Students are asked to appraise the justice of the means used to attain rapid industrialization in Russia.

Discuss problem of ends and means in other contexts, encouraging students to suggest goals worthy of any means.

Discuss the threats of totalitarianism within the United States as such threats relate to the dilemma of ends and means.

Lead students to state the generalization.

Estimated time required for this lesson: one day

Generalization No. 8

The type of totalitarianism which develops in a country is conditioned primarily by that nation's unique historical experience. The nature of the ideology, the level of economic development, and the degree of democratic experience are significant factors in explaining the origins and development of any totalitarian state.

This century has witnessed the appearance of a number of totalitarian states. Each has shared common features with the others: an ideology, a single mass party, strong leaders, a command economy, and the subordination of social institutions to the will of the political elite. Yet, within each of these categories, totalitarian nations have differed in kind as well as degree. Fascism differs from communism. Even when comparing Communist nations with each other, one can detect significant differences in the way their economies are organized, the authority of political leaders, the relationship with private institutions such as established churches, and in the varying interpretations of Communist ideology. By and large these differences result from differing cultural and historical experiences as well as the varying needs and crises each country must meet.

Despite the importance of unique, national, historical experiences, certain conditions have contributed to the rise of totalitarianism in the twentieth century. Political, social, and economic factors have not operated equally in each nation, but they can shed some light on the common origins of totalitarianism.

It is apparent that corruption and inefficiency in Chiang Kai-shek's government plus Chiang's inability to stop runaway inflation alienated many of the politically neutral populace and led them to throw their lot with the Communists. In Italy, displeasure with the corruption of politicians and fear caused by poverty and unemployment led the Italian people to accept the growth of militarism and regimentation. In Germany, defeat in World War I, reparations, depression, dissatisfaction with the Weimar government, and fear of communism caused many Germans to give their allegiance to the Nazis, although relatively few Germans supported specific Nazi objectives in the beginning. In Russia, it was military defeat in World War I, rural poverty, urban famine, and a corrupt tsarist government which gave the Bolsheviks sufficient support to seize and maintain power. In each of the four examples, experience in democratic government was limited. Moreover, in all of these countries, the people were not even agreed that democratic government was the most desirable type of political system.

The political unrest bubbling in Italy, Germany, and Russia at the turn of the twentieth century boiled over in the aftermath of World War I. Dissatisfaction with existing political systems grew as economic conditions worsened. Citizens looked to parties, to leaders who seemed to have the answers to their problems, leaders who seemed to offer a way out of their political and economic difficulties. Both Fascist and Communist regimes have gained power by harnessing the forces of public discontent.

Although both Fascist and Communist totalitarianism emerge in an atmosphere of political unrest, it appears that the growth of one or the other may depend upon the state of economic development the country has achieved before the period of crisis. Germany and Italy were on the road to industrialization; China and Russia were mostly agrarian societies. As a consequence, some students of totalitarianism argue that in periods of severe crisis, dissatisfied citizens in economically advanced countries are likely to turn to fascism, whereas in underdeveloped or newly developing countries, communism is more apt to gain hold.

SUGGESTED PROCEDURE

Because each totalitarian state gives an individual perspective to the overall pattern, it is suggested that students prepare reports on economic and political conditions in Italy, Germany, the Soviet Union, and China prior to the rise of the totalitarian regime. The reports would cover the following topics: economic conditions in Italy from 1919-1925, in Germany from 1919-1932, in Russia from 1914-1924, and in mainland China during the 1930's and 1940's; political conditions in the same countries during the same years. Since there would be eight reports in all, you may wish to arrange for committees of three or four students to prepare each of the reports. Students may draw from the bibliography which appears in Ebenstein or from the list of sources contained in Chapter III of this guide. If the following books are available in your school library, students will find them helpful for specific reports: Germany, *The Rise and Fall of the Third Reich*,[20] Chapters 2, 3, and 4; and *The Anatomy of Nazism*.[21] Italy: *Mussolini and Italian Fascism*.[22] Also Ignazio Silone's novel, *Bread and Wine*[23] describes political and economic conditions in Italy. For China see *Spotlight on Asia*,[24] Chapters 3, 9, and 10. The first chapter in *How Russia Is Ruled*[25] is useful for describing political, social, and economic conditions in Russia around the time of the 1917 revolution.

Student reports to the class can provide invaluable experience in research and oral presentation; such reports can also be boring, inaccurate, and ineffectual use of class time. We suggest that both the teacher and the students might get the most mileage out of these reports if they are carefully examined by the teacher before they are presented to the class, and if the class discussions focus

---

[20] William L. Shirer. *The Rise and Fall of the Third Reich: A History of Nazi Germany*. New York: Simon and Schuster, 1960.

[21] Earl Raab. *The Anatomy of Nazism*. New York: The Anti-Defamation League of B'nai B'rith, 1961. (The Anti-Defamation League, 315 Lexington Avenue, New York City has also produced a filmstrip, *Anatomy of Nazism*.)

[22] S. William Halperin. *Mussolini and Italian Fascism*. Princeton, N.J.; Anvil Books, D. Van Nostrand Company, Inc., 1964.

[23] Ignazio Silone. *Bread and Wine*. New York: Signet Books, The New American Library of World Literature, Inc., 1959.

[24] Guy Wint. *Spotlight on Asia*. Baltimore: Penguin Books, Inc., 1959.

[25] Merle Fainsod. *How Russia Is Ruled*. Cambridge: Harvard University Press, 1963.

sharply on the points raised in the reports. Each report should describe the specific conditions operating in the nation. The class may attempt to generalize from the unique experiences.

The political reports can be presented first, each individual report being followed by class discussion of the political characteristics of the country described. Specific questions which students ought to consider in their political reports are: What experience had the general public had in democratic government at the time the leader of the totalitarian regime seized power? How many political parties were active in the country? How violently did these political parties disagree among themselves? How much interest did the average citizen take in political affairs? What was the strength of forces on the left? On the right? Why did some people want to restore the monarchy which had been powerful before the world war?

After all four political reports have been presented, the class should be led to form generalizations about political conditions common to all four countries. For example, the political institutions in each country were in a state of disintegration; the populace had had limited experience in self-government; both organized political parties and pressure groups or elements fought among themselves for control; and there was conflict about the goals of the society as well as about the means which should be used to achieve any goals.

A similar procedure can be followed for the economic reports, but the class discussion after all four reports have been presented should bring out the differences between the Communist and Fascist experiences as well as the similarities. The thesis that the kind of totalitarianism which emerges—either totalitarianism of the right, fascism, or totalitarianism of the left, communism—appears to be related to the relative stage of economic development can be subjected to the scrutiny of the class. Do the reports support this theory?

Questions which can be raised in their economic reports are: What effect did war have on the economy of the country? How industrialized was the country before the war? Just after the war? Was the country advanced or underdeveloped in its economy prior to the establishment of a totalitarian regime? How was the economy affected by the depression of the thirties? What is inflation? How does inflation affect entrepreneurs? How does it affect individuals who live on fixed wages and salaries?

Did Hitler receive his early support from blue collar workers? White collar workers? From industrialists? From small businessmen? From the intelligentsia? What groups supported the Communists in their early days?

PSYCHOLOGICAL FACTORS

The severity of political and economic crises confronting such countries as Nazi Germany and Soviet Russia does not fully account for the rise of totalitarianism. Students might well ask why other nations confronted with similar problems found other solutions. One important factor in the rise of totalitarianism is the presence of a strong leader, capable of attracting public loyalty during the period of crisis and maintaining his control over all military and civil elements in the country after the general public has surrendered to the domination of the regime. As students have seen in Generalization No. 5 of this guide, leaders in totalitarian states are glorified and regarded as superhuman beings. The fact that totalitarian leaders have been able to capture and control all power centers in the nation or the fact that totalitarian leaders appear to have all the answers—these facts alone do not account for the charismatic qualities of totalitarian leadership; as Ebenstein points out (p. 71), "No social and political system . . . is ever much better or much worse than the people who operate and live under it. For every big Hitler there must be many little Hitlers in a nation, just as for every Jefferson to succeed there must be many small Jeffersons at the same time."

Psychological factors play an important part in the totalitarian leader's rise to power. On one hand, the leader has the genius to identify and capture the vital forces of the society; on the other hand, many people in the society want the leader to control them. In a film prepared by the U.S. Air Force in 1948 (*The Communist Weapon of Allure*), Dr. Warren B. Walsh points out that totalitarianism appeals to four basic needs in man, needs which recede or become dominant according to the fluctuations of other aspects of man's existence. These are the needs to belong, for recognition, to lead, and to be led. People come to want a totalitarian leader when they feel incompetent to make their own decisions, when they no longer want to make their own decisions, or when they want to become identified with a cause larger than themselves or their immediate society, or when they seek a channel through which they can control their fellow human beings.

Several students may wish to prepare reports on the psychological aspects of totalitarianism. In *Escape from Freedom*,[26] Erich Fromm considers the difficulties of the autonomous individual, pointing out why many people find it easier to accept authorities who will completely regulate their lives. The appeals of mass movements, the types of people who are potential fanatics, the techniques used by leaders of mass movements are among the topics considered by Eric Hoffer in *The True Believer*.[27] Mr. Hoffer notes that "A rising mass movement attracts and holds a following not by its doctrine and promises but by the refuge it offers from the anxieties, barrenness and meaninglessness of an individual existence. It cures the poignantly frustrated not by conferring on them an absolute truth or by remedying the difficulties and abuses which made their lives miserable, but by freeing them from their ineffectual selves—and it does this by enfolding and absorbing them into a closely knit and exultant corporate whole."

An effective means of pulling together and reinforcing knowledge of the political, economic and psychological factors which contribute to the rise of totalitarianism is by showing the film, *The Twisted Cross*.[28] Because *The Twisted Cross* is an hour long, we suggest that it be shown in two class periods. The first five minutes of class time could be devoted to telling students the things they should look for in the film; the time after the film can be used to discuss the points made in the film. There is, if time permits, considerable advantage in discussing the film while it is

---

[26] Erich Fromm. *Escape from Freedom*. New York: Holt, Rinehart, and Winston, 1941.
[27] Eric Hoffer. *The True Believer*. New York: Mentor Books, The New American Library of World Literature, Inc., 1961.
[28] *The Twisted Cross*, which was first presented on NBC television, may be rented from a number of film libraries or purchased from McGraw-Hill, Inc.

still fresh in the minds of the students rather than waiting until the next day.

As students watch *The Twisted Cross*, they should look for information about the economic and political conditions in the Weimar Republic when Hitler came to power. The early part of the film notes the crises which confronted Germany after World War I. Then, the film describes the appeals which Nazism made to the German people: the attraction of a mass movement—the sense of belonging, the answers offered by the Nazi leader, the religious aspects of Nazi ideology. Students might note especially the use of band music and marching, the use of crowds to attract more crowds, which inspire an urge literally to "fall into step."

In the second section of the film, students should note the general characteristics of totalitarian regimes: attacks on internal and external "enemies" of the state, glorification of the leader, persuasion through propaganda and simple slogans, persuasion through terror, and finally the expansionist tendencies leading to war.

The film may also be used to help students better understand each of the generalizations that have been made throughout the guide by observing these generalizations practiced in Nazi Germany. Such a use of the film may be valuable as a culminating activity of its own or as a bridge to the final lesson described in this guide. Before the film is shown, the students should be asked to list each of the guide's basic generalizations in their notebooks. As they watch the film, they can note specific instances in which they observe the generalization at work. After each half of the film, the teacher may ask students to describe the examples they have listed for each generalization. In this way the film becomes a valuable teaching instrument.

Outline of Lesson Plan

Eight committees formed. Topics assigned.

Reports reviewed by teacher.

Four political reports, each followed by class discussion.

Comparison and analysis of all four reports.

Four economic reports, each followed by class discussion.

Comparison and analysis of economic reports.

Formulation of Generalization 8.

Optional: Assignment and discussion of psychological factors.

Film: *The Twisted Cross*. Part I, followed by discussion. Part II followed by discussion.

Estimated time required for this lesson: one to four days depending upon the inclusion of optional activities.

Generalization No. 9

Totalitarianism is a political, social and economic system which uses any means available to subject the individual to the goals and leadership of the state.

The object of this guide has been to introduce students to various aspects of totalitarianism through a series of generalizations. Conceptual models are constructed somewhat as the pieces cf a jig-saw puzzle are put together. We have avoided asking students to verbalize their understanding of totalitarianism, fearing that premature verbalization of the concept might block a further building of the model in their own minds.

Now that students have had an opportunity to examine various aspects of totalitarianism and consider some of the implications which arise from these aspects, they should be prepared to define their model, to verbalize their conception. Students who understand the meaning of totalitarianism should also be able to use the concept analytically as a model with which to examine contemporary political and social systems. Furthermore, while achieving a more complete understanding of totalitarianism, they may also have gained a better comprehension of democracy.

Suggested Procedure

Ask each student to write his own definition of totalitarianism as a homework assignment. The definitions will be given to you at the beginning of the period on the following day. The definition should be brief, but include the principal ideas contained in each of the generalizations. Limit the students to two or three sentences or a maximum of 50 words. This will prevent a student from simply adding all the generalizations together and calling this his definition. It is very important that each student be required to do this assignment individually. Only by reading his verbalization of the concept, can you be certain that he has captured the full meaning of the term totalitarianism.

After you have gathered up the individual definitions of totalitarianism at the beginning of the class period, you may wish to divide the class into several discussion groups and suggest that each group prepare a definition of totalitarianism. The discussion which ensues should further refine students' understanding of the concept. Allow 15 to 20 minutes for the group discussions and then call for the group reports.

As each group reports its definition of totalitarianism, write it on the board. After all definitions have been reported to the class, try to lead the class to a single definition of totalitarianism. The striving for consensus will not be satisfying to all, since some students will see their words changed to accommodate the views of others. Nevertheless such a process yields opportunities to force students to be precise in their language. Furthermore, you can make a final check on the understanding of specific generalizations. For example, if a student insists that "one-party state" must somehow be included in the definition, ask him what the phrase, "one-party state," means. Are all nation-states which have but a single, powerful party necessarily totalitarian?

While the attempt in class to lead students to agreement on a single definition of totalitarianism is a useful exercise for the purposes outlined above, a better test of whether individual students understand the concept appears in the definitions each student constructed in the homework assignment.

Finally, whether the concept has really become an intellectual tool for each student, providing him with a measure for analyzing political and social systems, can only be validated by observing his behavior when the opportunities for such analyses arise. Therefore, in order to evaluate the degree to which the concept of totalitarianism has become operative for your students, give each student a case study or a descriptive account of a contemporary nation-state and ask that he write a paper in which he applies his model of totalitarianism to this society, noting at which points the society does or does not conform to his model. Peggy Durdin's pamphlet, *Mao's China*,[29] is ideal for such purposes. Requiring that students demonstrate their comprehension through application is the most satisfactory way to discover what they have learned from this unit.

Outline of Lesson Plan

Each student prepares his own definition of totalitarianism.

Students work in small groups to formulate a group definition of totalitarianism.

Write group definitions on the board and try to arrive at a consensus on a single definition of totalitarianism.

Follow-up activity:
Assign a case study or descriptive account of a contemporary nation-state, asking each student to write a paper in which he applies his model of totalitarianism to this nation-state.

Estimated time for this lesson: one to five days depending upon the use of the follow-up activity.

---

[29] Peggy Durdin. *Mao's China*. Headline Series, Foreign Policy Association, 136 (July-August, 1959).

CHAPTER III

Suggestions For
Further Reading

While the purpose of this guide is primarily to describe one approach to teaching about totalitarianism, brief mention should be made of other references teachers can check to supplement this unit or to plan their own units. The following list notes *general sources* for teachers who are planning units for their classes and *specialized references* for teachers and better students. There has been no attempt to make the list complete; what follows are only selected samples of the abundant fare that is available.

SOURCES FOR PLANNING UNITS RELATING TO TOTALITARIANISM

Since communism is the most significant totalitarian movement today, there are many sources available for teaching about communism. There is relatively little in print about other totalitarian systems. An exception is *The Third Reich in Perspective: A Resource Unit for Teachers and Group Leaders* available from the Anti-Defamation League of B'nai B'rith, 315 Lexington Avenue, New York City.

Richard M. Perdew, a high school teacher, has published in *Social Education* 38 (February, 1964) a detailed list of materials for teaching about communism and the Soviet Union. The Service Center for Teachers of the American Historical Association has published three pamphlets which provide helpful bibliographies for teachers preparing units on communism. They are: *Marxism Since the Communist Manifesto* by Alfred G. Meyer, *Russia Since 1917* by George Barr Carson, Jr., and *Forty Years of Chinese*

Communism: Selected Readings with Commentary by Allan B. Cole. They may be purchased from The Macmillan Company, New York.

Useful suggestions to guide high school teachers in organizing and presenting materials on communism are found in each of the following: American Bar Association, *Instruction on Communism and Its Contrast with Liberty under Law.* Chicago: American Bar Association, 1962; American Legion and National Education Association, Joint Committee, *Teaching about Communism—Guidelines for Junior and Senior High Schools.* Indianapolis: Americanism Commission of the American Legion, 1962; Merrill F. Hartshorn, and T. Marcus Gillespie, *Selected Annotated Bibliography to Assist Teachers in Teaching About Communism.* Washington: The National Council for the Social Studies, 1962; and *Teaching about Communism and Democracy: Case Studies.* Chicago: Institute for American Strategy, 1961. A valuable handbook which has been prepared for teachers is *Democracy and Totalitarianism: A Handbook for Teachers,* ed. by Robert E. de Jong. St. Louis: Educational Council for Responsible Citizenship, 1962. A discussion of the problem of teaching about communism and a description of some practices throughout the United States is provided by David Mallery, *Teaching About Communism.* Boston: National Association of Independent Schools, 1962. In addition, many states and some school systems have prepared their own guides for teaching about totalitarianism.

The market contains a number of textbooks that have been designed for high school students studying units or courses on communism or on specific communist nations. Space does not permit listing them all, but two are suggested as being of potential interest to teachers. One is E. Raymond Platig, *The United States and the Soviet Challenge.* Chicago: NCA Foreign Relations Project and Laidlaw Brothers, 1965; the other is *Communism in Theory and Practice,* ed. by Howard D. Mehlinger. San Francisco: Chandler Publishing Company, 1964. The latter book contains readings which may be used by teachers in a way similar to that followed in this guide.

Special mention must be given to a teaching guide that is indirectly related to the study of totalitarianism. This is a unit by

Robert Hanvey entitled *The Idea of Liberty in American Culture,* Anthropology Curriculum Study Project, 1963. Teachers who have become interested in teaching concepts inductively will find Hanvey's guide especially valuable.

SPECIAL REFERENCES

There are a number of books that deal with the general phenomena of totalitarianism. William Ebenstein, *Totalitarianism: New Perspectives.* New York: Holt, Rinehart, and Winston, Inc., 1962 is the book upon which the present guide was based. Ebenstein's *Today's Isms: Communism, Fascism, Capitalism, Socialism,* 4th ed., Englewood Cliffs, N.J.: Prentice-Hall, 1964, is used as a textbook in secondary schools and college classrooms. Carl J. Friedrich and Zbigniew K. Brzezinski in *Totalitarian Dictatorship and Autocracy,* New York: Frederick A. Praeger, 1956, treat the general development of modern totalitarianism. Friedrich is also the editor of *Totalitarianism,* New York: Grossett and Dunlap, 1964, which contains the contributions of a number of scholars on the topic.

Teachers interested in using readings on totalitarianism in the classroom should see *Communism, Fascism, and Democracy: The Theoretical Foundations,* ed. by Carl Cohen, New York: Random House, 1962, and *Dictatorship and Totalitarianism: Selected Readings,* ed. by Betty Brand Burch, Princeton, N.J.: Anvil Books, D. Van Nostrand, Inc., 1964.

Among the books which provide excellent treatments of Fascism and Nazism are: William Ebenstein, *Fascist Italy.* New York: American Book Company, 1939; William Ebenstein, *The Nazi State.* New York: Holt, Rinehart and Winston, 1943; M. Baumont and others, *The Third Reich.* New York: Frederick A. Praeger, 1955; William L. Shirer, *The Rise and Fall of the Third Reich: A History of Nazi Germany.* New York: Simon and Schuster, 1960; and Earl Raab, *The Anatomy of Nazism.* Anti-Defamation League of B'nai B'rith, 1961. Those teachers wishing to use readings may find S. William Halperin, *Mussolini and Italian Fascism,* Princeton, N.J.: Anvil Books, D. Van Nostrand,

Inc., 1964, and Eugen Weber, *Varieties of Fascism: Doctrines of Revolution in the Twentieth Century*, Princeton, N.J.: Anvil Books, D. Van Nostrand, Inc., 1964, especially useful.

Two books that explore the psychological factors that seem to attract men toward totalitarian solutions are Erich Fromm, *Escape from Freedom*. New York: Holt, Rinehart, and Winston, 1941; and Eric Hoffer, *The True Believer: Thoughts on the Nature of Mass Movements*, Mentor Books, The New American Library, 1951.

The literature on communism is indeed vast. Therefore, only a few titles from the many books that are available can be cited. An excellent overall treatment of communism is Alfred G. Meyer, *Communism*. New York: Random House, 1960. The introductory chapter is useful to the teacher preparing to explain the functions of ideology to his class. A book which describes clearly and concisely the operations of the Soviet economic system is Robert W. Campbell, *Soviet Economic Power*. New York: Houghton Mifflin, 1960. Merle Fainsod's book *How Russia Is Ruled*, Cambridge: Harvard University Press, 1963, remains a basic text on the Soviet political system. Two books that provide interesting interpretations of the Soviet system are John N. Hazard, *The Soviet System of Government*, Chicago: University of Chicago Press, rev. ed. 1960; and Zbigniew Brzezinski and Samuel P. Huntington, *Political Power: USA/USSR*. New York: The Viking Press, 1964. Hazard believes the Soviet political apparatus can best be understood "if it is described as incorporating democratic forms, counterweighted with totalitarian controls." Huntington and Brzezinski compare and contrast the role of leadership and the process of decision-making in the United States and the Soviet Union. An interesting book that contains accounts by former Communists and Communist sympathizers and which describes why they first joined, then deserted communism is *The God that Failed*, ed. by Richard Crossman. New York: Bantam Books, 1952.

Teachers may wish to explore elements of totalitarianism in American life. An excellent description of the origins of the American Communist Party is Theodore Draper, *The Roots of American Communism*, New York: The Viking Press, 1957. A general treatment of the American party may be found in Irving

Howe and Lewis Coser, *The American Communist Party: A Critical History*. New York: Frederick A. Praeger, 1962. For a discussion of totalitarianism of the right in American life, see Arnold Forster and Benjamin R. Epstein, *Danger on the Right*, New York: Random House, 1964; *The Radical Right*, ed. by Daniel Bell, Garden City, N.Y.: Anchor Books, Doubleday and Company, Inc., 1963; and Harry and Bonaro Overstreet, *The Strange Tactics of Extremism*, New York: W. W. Norton, 1964.

Many teachers have found the use of fiction to be an excellent device for helping students gain more than just a surface impression of a topic. George Orwell's *1984*, New York: Harcourt, Brace & World, 1949, remains the classic account of a totalitarian model while his *Animal Farm*, New York: Harcourt, Brace & World, 1946, is a satire on modern totalitarianism, using animals in place of people. In *Darkness at Noon*, New York: The Macmillan Company, 1941, Arthur Koestler has recaptured much of the drama and emotion which marked the Soviet purge trials of the 1930's. These three works are also available in paperback editions (Signet Classics, New American Library). In *Bread and Wine*, New York: Signet Book, The New American Library, 1959, Ignazio Silone describes conditions in Italy which drew Italians into both Fascist and Communist movements. And finally, a book which contains nine fictitious, but highly representative, sketches of Soviet citizens during the time of Stalin is Raymond A. Bauer, *Nine Soviet Portraits*, Cambridge: Massachusetts Institute of Technology and Wiley, 1955.

SELECTED PUBLICATIONS
OF THE NATIONAL COUNCIL FOR THE SOCIAL STUDIES
1201 Sixteenth St., N.W., Washington, D.C. 20036

Yearbooks

Thirty-Fifth Yearbook (1965), *Evaluation in Social Studies*, Harry D. Berg, editor, $4.00; cloth $5.00

Thirty-Fourth Yearbook (1964), *New Perspectives in World History*, Shirley H. Engle, editor, $5.00; cloth $6.00

Thirty-Third Yearbook (1963), *Skill Development in Social Studies*, Helen Mc-Cracken Carpenter, editor. $4.00; cloth $5.00

Thirty-Second Yearbook (1962), *Social Studies in Elementary Schools*, John U. Michaelis, editor. $4.00; cloth $5.00

Thirty-First Yearbook (1961), *Interpreting and Teaching American History*, William H. Cartwright and Richard L. Watson, Jr., co-editors. $4.00; cloth $5.00

Bulletins

Bulletin No. 36 (1965), *Social Studies Curriculum Improvement: A Guide for Local Committees*, Raymond H. Muessig, editor. $2.00

Bulletin No. 35 (1964), *Improving the Teaching of World Affairs: The Glens Falls Story*, by Harold M. Long and Robert N. King. $2.00

Bulletin No. 34 (1963), *Guiding the Social Studies Reading of High School Students*, by Ralph C. Preston, J. Wesley Schneyer, and Franc J. Thyng. $1.50

Bulletin No. 15 (rev. ed. 1964), *Selected Items for the Testing of Study Skills and Critical Thinking*, by Horace T. Morse and George H. McCune. $1.50

Bulletin No. 9 (rev. ed. 1960), *Selected Test Items in World History*, by H. R. Anderson and E. F. Lindquist. Revised by David K. Heenan. $1.50

Bulletin No. 6 (rev. ed. 1964), *Selected Test Items in American History*, by H. R. Anderson and E. F. Lindquist. Revised by Harriet Stull. $1.50

Curriculum Series

Number 11 (1961), *Selected Resource Units: Elementary Social Studies, Kindergarten-Grade Six*, Wilhelmina Hill, editor. $2.25

Number 7 (rev. ed. 1965), *Social Studies in the Senior High School: Programs for Grades Ten, Eleven, and Twelve*, Willis D. Moreland, editor. $2.25

Number 6 (rev. ed. 1957), *Social Studies for the Junior High School: Programs for Grades Seven, Eight, and Nine*, Julian C. Aldrich, editor. $2.00

Number 5 (new ed. 1960), *Social Studies for the Middle Grades: Answering Teachers' Questions*, C. W. Hunnicutt, editor. $2.25.

NOTE: *Orders which amount to $2.00 or less must be accompanied by cash.* Postage will be prepaid on cash orders, but orders not accompanied by cash will be billed with postage charges included. A complete publications list will be sent free on request.